·RED ROCK·
SACRED MOUNTAIN

the Canyons & Peaks from Sedona to Flagstaff

STEWART AITCHISON
FOREWORD BY JAMES E. BABBITT

Voyageur Press

For Wild Bill

Edited by Kathy Mallien

Printed in Hong Kong
92 93 94 95 96 5 4 3 2 1

Library of Congress Cataloging-in-Publication Data

Aitchison, Stewart M.
Red Rock–Sacred Mountain : the canyons and peaks from Sedona to Flagstaff / Stewart Aitchison.
p. cm.
Incluces bibliographical references and index.
ISBN 0-89658-215-9
1. Natural history–Arizona–Sedona Region. 2. Natural history–Arizona–Flagstaff Region. Human ecology–Arizona–Sedona Region. 4. Human ecology–Arizona–Flagstaff Region. 5. Indians of North America–Arizona–Sedona Region. 6. Indians of North America–Arizona–Flagstaff Region. I. Title.
QH105.A65A375 1992
508.791'33–dc20
92-19896
CIP

Published by
VOYAGEUR PRESS, INC.
P.O. Box 338, 123 North Second Street
Stillwater, MN 55082 U.S.A.
From Minnesota and Canada 612-430-2210
Toll-free 800-888-9653

Voyageur Press books are also available at discounts for quantities for educational, fundraising, premium, or sales-promotion use. For details contact the marketing department. Please write or call for our free catalog of natural history publications.

Front cover: View of the San Francisco Peaks. Back cover: Cathedral Rock from Red Rock Crossing.

Page 1: The stunning beauty of the Red Rock–Sacred Mountain landscape no doubt struck a cord in the hearts and minds of those first ancient hunters who wandered through here thousands of years ago, just as it does for the modern visitor. Through the ages, people have continually found inspiration among the red cliffs and snowy peaks.

CONTENTS

FOREWORD

Dᴜʀɪɴɢ ᴛʜᴇ ᴡɪɴᴛᴇʀ of 1979, I moved with my wife and son back to Flagstaff from northern California where we had lived for several years. Coming back to the snow and cold weather was easy for me since I was born and raised in Flagstaff. The transition to an alpine climate was considerably more difficult for my wife and son, both California natives.

We decided to head south to the Sedona area as often as possible that winter to escape the chill and enjoy weekend hikes in a warmer climate. I came across a small book written in 1978 by Stewart Aitchison which proved invaluable on our weekend treks. Over the next few months, that book opened up a whole new world of information about the natural history of the Red Rock Country, and re-introduced us to one of the most spectacular scenic areas of the Southwest. The author's first book, *Oak Creek Canyon and the Red Rock Country of Arizona: A Natural History and Trail Guide*, occupies a special place in my library.

Its author has since produced other works on the natural history of northern Arizona and southern Utah, leading to the present volume, *Red Rock–Sacred Mountain*. These writings all reflect Aitchison's exhaustive knowledge of the biology, geology, archaeology, and history of our region. Perhaps more importantly, they convey his love of the natural environment and his deep concern for its preservation and protection.

Aitchison's latest book challenges the reader to think about the impact of human activity on our local environment. Dramatic changes have occurred in the landscape even in the relatively short period since Flagstaff's settlement in the 1880s. Early photographs reveal very different patterns in the growth and distribution of forests and grasslands than exist today. Apparently, more abundant surface waters observed by early explorers have disappeared. Wildlife also has felt the effect of our presence over the past century. The implications of these changes are not fully known. It is clear that we all must reflect on these issues and help to develop a new balance between humans and their natural environment. We have reason to thank the author for another very special book–one that enhances our appreciation of the San Francisco Peaks–Red Rock region and causes us to be concerned about the future of our natural heritage.

James E. Babbitt, Flagstaff, Arizona, February 1992

INTRODUCTION

AUTUMN 1965. MY COLLEGE roommate dropped me off on the Schultz Pass Road near the old golf course just north of Flagstaff. Strapped on my back was a smelly, army-surplus, chicken-feather sleeping bag, a heavy olive-drab tarp, a little food, a can of Sterno, and a saddle blanket–covered canteen. I was ready to conquer the San Francisco Peaks.

The sharp summit of Agassiz pierced the azure sky and beckoned to me. I began my march directly toward the peak, determined this time to make it to the top. Just a week before, my first attempt had been aborted because of rain and my total ineptness at rigging shelter out of a tarp.

Onward I walked, squeezing through thickets of tightly packed pines, then through open stands of orange-barked ponderosas, and occasionally across grassy meadows bordered with aspens, some carved with names and dates: Pedro Azmanez 1921; José Acosta 1938; Manuel Silva 1935; Joe Gallegos. At the time, I didn't know that these deep, gray-outlined scars in the white aspen bark had probably been left by Basque sheepherders. Nor did I realize that if I had stayed on the Schultz Pass Road and then followed the Weatherford Road instead of heading cross-country that my way to the summit ridge would have been much less arduous. In those days, I had more gumption than common sense.

As the sun set, I found myself still well below timberline and crossing a rather steep slope. Being totally ignorant about proper campsites and not wanting to lose any of my hard-gained altitude, I chose to camp right where I stood. The only problem with that was that my sleeping bag kept creeping downhill all night!

Very early the next morning, I packed up my things and started once again for the top. The trees became stunted and fewer in number and then finally disappeared altogether as I climbed. My heart was pounding with each step, my breathing labored . . . was I going to have a heart attack? Such silly thoughts ran through the mind of a novice mountaineer from the flatlands of Illinois.

Finally, I dragged myself the last few rocky steps to the summit of Agassiz. Off to the north was the higher peak of Humphreys. To me, in my exhausted state, it looked a million miles away. But the expansive view across forest and desert was extraordinary.

Much to my surprise, I saw a ski lift below me on the west slope of Agassiz. After an unsuccessful attempt at cooking powdered chicken noodle soup at twelve thousand feet with a little can of Sterno, I descended to the ski lift terminal.

The lift was running for scenic rides. The attendant was so surprised to see me coming down from the summit that he asked if I would like a free ride down to the ski lodge. I gladly accepted, physically pooped but mentally exhilarated from the climb.

A few evenings later I was riding with my roommate John to his home in Cottonwood. We drove south of Flagstaff on Highway 89A and soon began the twisting, curving descent into Oak Creek Canyon. Here was the scene straight out of Zane Grey's *Call of the Canyon:* "The very forest-fringed earth seemed to have opened into a deep abyss, ribbed by red rock walls and choked by mats of green timber. . . . What a wild, lonely, terrible place. . . . This insulated rift in the crust of the earth was a gigantic burrow for beasts, perhaps for outlawed

The view of Cathedral Rock from Red Rock Crossing has been the backdrop for many western movies and has become the classic symbol of the Red Rock Country.

men – not for a civilized person. . . . "

We had encountered no traffic, no outlaws, and no beasts except for a ringtail cat that darted across the highway, so John turned off the car's headlights. A full moon lit our way almost as brightly as street lights. We stopped several times to enjoy the nighttime view. Stars winked in the black velvet sky and the red rocks glowed from within. It was a magical, overwhelming, enthralling night.

The Red Rock Country and Sacred Mountain had stolen my heart and inflamed my curiosity. This beautiful, wondrous place was to become my home, my safe harbor to return to whenever I tentatively explored the "outside" world. The Peaks greet me each morning, and I can escape twentieth-century pressures by hiking the Red Rock wilderness.

Since those early days, I have become an insatiable student of this region. This book encompasses Sedona, Flagstaff, Oak Creek Canyon, and the San Francisco Peaks – essentially the Coconino National Forest. These place-names may not be household words, but millions of people would readily recognize the landscapes of this area as the backgrounds in countless horse operas, TV commercials, and magazine ads. Each year millions of tourists visit Oak Creek Canyon, a major corridor between these two towns. Millions more pass through Flagstaff on their way to the Grand Canyon or traversing Interstate 40 coming or going from California and points east.

The emphasis of this book is diverse natural history of the Red Rock Country and the San Francisco Peaks, although many of the concepts and ideas extend far beyond the immediate area. Contrary to popular notion, Arizona, particularly the north-central part of the state, is not all desert. First-time visitors are always amazed to learn that the largest contiguous ponderosa pine forest in the world surrounds Flagstaff, which itself sits atop a high plateau that averages seven thousand feet above sea level. From Sedona to the summit of the San Francisco Peaks, one travels from desert grassland to alpine tundra. This horizontal distance of about thirty-five miles is comparable, biologically, to going from Mexico to Canada. Additionally, the biological panoply is set upon some of the most gorgeous scenery (read as fantastic geology) in the American Southwest.

The human history of this area is as unique and varied as its geology. Thus, I've devoted a couple of chapters to prehistoric cultures and the early European explorers who were later followed by government surveyors and scientists.

As you read this book, remember that the Red Rock–Sacred Mountain region is not inviolate. In the past, too many picture books have expounded the natural wonders and beauty without indicating that numerous threats, a few obvious, many insidious, endanger the land and its inhabitants. I have tried to follow E. B. White's advice: "One role of the writer today is to sound the alarm. The environment is disintegrating, the hour is late, and not much is being done." Here I have attempted to sound the alarm about some of the environmental dilemmas facing us. Please join me on a brief natural history tour of the Red Rock–Sacred Mountain area, and consider what can be done to preserve this astonishing region.

7

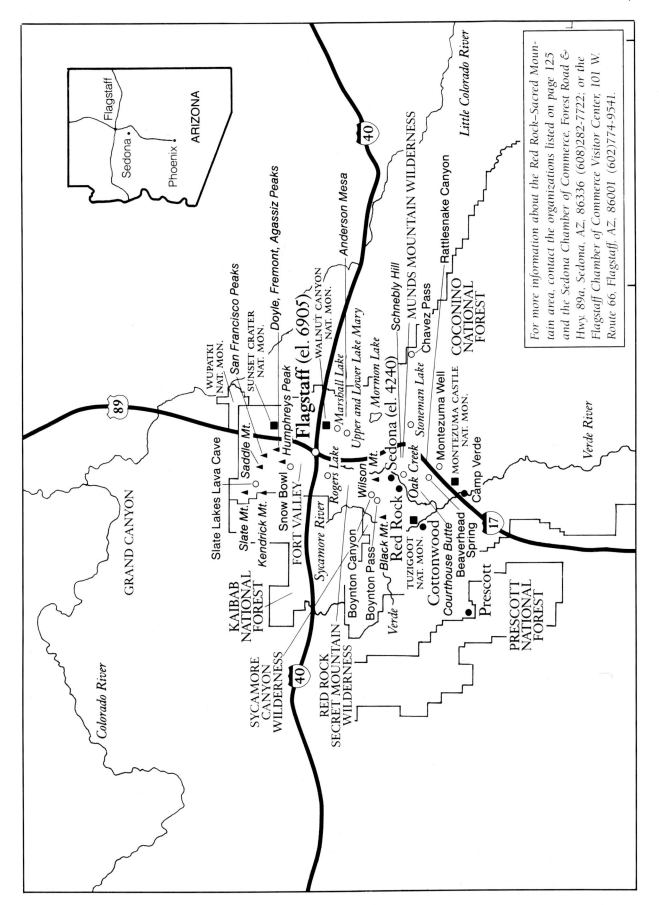

For more information about the Red Rock–Sacred Mountain area, contact the organizations listed on page 125 and the Sedona Chamber of Commerce, Forest Road & Hwy. 89a, Sedona, AZ, 86336 (608)282-7722; or the Flagstaff Chamber of Commerce Visitor Center, 101 W. Route 66, Flagstaff, AZ, 86001 (602)774-9541.

ANCIENT SEAS
AND LAVA RIVERS

IREACH THE 12,633-FOOT crown of Humphreys Peak just as the sun emerges above the eastern horizon. Humphreys is only one of several high points along the rim of this extinct volcano, a mountain sacred to the Hopi and Navajo and known today as the San Francisco Peaks. This highest summit in Arizona was named after Brigadier General Andrew A. Humphreys, a bureaucrat who directed government surveys from his Washington, D.C., office. Other points along the rim include Agassiz (12,356 feet), Fremont (11,969 feet), and Doyle (11,460 feet).

Agassiz, the peak that appears to be the highest when viewed from Flagstaff, was named for the renowned Swiss geologist, zoologist, and teacher from Harvard, Jean Louis Rodolphe Agassiz. Agassiz came west in 1868 to search for fossils and study geology along the Union Pacific

Railroad between Chicago and Green River, Wyoming. Like Humphreys, he never saw the San Francisco Peaks. Fremont, named after John C. Fremont, the so-called "Pathfinder of the West," is another sharp peak visible from town. Fremont was appointed Arizona territorial governor in 1878, but the closest he got to the Peaks was the town of Prescott. Doyle, the rounded summit to the east, is the only high point named after a local resident. Allen Doyle was a Flagstaff pioneer, stockman, and guide. He was also a good friend of novelist Zane Grey and became a prototype for the writer's fictional tough western heroes. Doyle built a horse trail up the mountain to Doyle Saddle.

The air this morning is cold and still. From this apex of Arizona, I have a grand 360-degree view of desert, forest, and canyon landscapes—landscapes that display millions of years of dynamic earth history.

To the distant north, the scene is one of relatively flat, succeeding and receding horizontal bands of pastel hues. These colorful layers of sedimentary stone retreat into the shallow valley carved by the Little Colorado River and then continue into the badlands of the Painted Desert, the sharp ridge of the Echo Cliffs, and the walls of a thousand hidden canyons, including the biggest of them all—the Grand.

Geologists have likened the progression of layers from the depths of the Grand Canyon to the high mesas and plateaus of southern Utah to a giant staircase ascending the geologic time scale. The oldest rocks are the bottom steps. As one climbs higher, the rock layers become younger and younger. The rock pages record a mind-boggling billion and a half years worth of earth history, today exposed by the downcutting of the mighty Colorado River and its myriad tributaries. This paradise for students of earth history is called the Colorado Plateau: a 130,000-square-mile chunk of canyon and mesa real estate that covers northern Arizona and parts of Utah, Colorado, and New Mexico.

To the south, the dark green, relatively flat, heavily forested land abruptly ends at the escarpment called the Mogollon Rim, a one- to two-thousand-foot leap into central Arizona's desert Verde Valley. The Rim also defines the southern boundary of the physiographic Colorado Plateau. Beyond the Verde Valley, a series of roughly parallel mountain ranges separated by more low desert valleys marches off into the distance. This is the Basin and Range Country.

The edge of the Mogollon Rim has been weakened by faults or breaks that have since been carved into deep canyons by flowing streams like Oak Creek, Sycamore, Wet Beaver, and Fossil. The brilliant vermilion sandstones and shales that have been revealed and further sculpted into mesas, buttes, and spires comprise the celebrated Red Rock Country.

Below me, closer at hand, the Peaks are surrounded by hundreds of small cinder cones, in various stages of erosional disrepair. Lava flows, most ancient and forest-cloaked, a few relatively new and raw, coat the local sedimentary rocks. Rising above the igneous veneer are a dozen or so larger volcanoes, but none of these igneous extrusions reach the magnitude and symmetry of the San Francisco Peaks—a sacred mountain to the Native Americans and more recent residents.

The Red Rock–Sacred Mountain area forms the geologic core of my home range and poses endless mysteries. The geologist in me seeks the answers to two basic questions: Where did these rocks come from, and how were they shaped into the remarkable landscapes I see today?

A whisper of a southwesterly breeze increases the rate of evaporation of my sweat-soaked shirt. A chill runs down my back. Time to put on another layer of clothing.

As I rest, I think back to my first summit climb more than twenty-five years ago. Today the land looks basically unchanged, save for the incursions of new buildings and roads. The mountains, the mesas, the canyons appear static, permanent. Even the relatively recent eruptions and lava flows associated with the nearby volcano called Sunset Crater seem timeless. On our human time scale, the temporal nature of the landscape is difficult to appreciate.

I can remember back to my youth, a time span measured in a few decades. I hear the stories told by my parents and grandparents and can juxtapose them with family photos and historical illustrations to get a feeling for events that happened in the last century. But then I read about prehistoric cultures or visit an archaeological site or view artifacts in a museum and try to conjure up a living, breathing civilization, and my poor brain is taxed. When it comes to thinking in terms of millions and billions of years, the concept is nearly impossible for me to grasp.

Where did these rocks come from? In a word, deposition—either as an accumulation of sediments transported by wind or water or by the eruption of hot, molten material from deep within the earth.

The oldest rocks exposed in the Flagstaff–Sedona area (keep in mind that these rocks presumably overlie yet older layers such as those seen in the depths of the nearby Grand Canyon) are marine limestones formed in a warm shallow sea during early to late Mississipian time, about 330 million years ago.

This layer is known as the Redwall Limestone, a name referring to the reddish coating of iron oxides that gets washed down from red sandstones overlying this formation. The rock's true color is an off-white to grayish blue, and was called the Blue Lime by early prospectors.

The Redwall underlies all of the Red Rock Country but outcrops only in lower Dry Creek and at the mouth of Sycamore Canyon. The total thickness of the Redwall in this area is unknown but probably is comparable to the four hundred to six hundred feet observed in the Grand Canyon. In some earlier geologic reports, the Redwall was reported from Oak Creek Canyon, but those exposed limey deposits are now considered to be the bottom layer of the younger, overlying Supai Group.

As time went on, the ocean floor slowly began to rise. The shoreline migrated westerly. Other sediments may have been deposited on top of the Redwall, but eventually the newly exposed land was attacked by erosion. Any

This unusual pattern in the sandstone walls of Woods Canyon within the Munds Mountain Wilderness Area may be related to joints (vertical fractures) formed when the region began to be uplifted 65 million years ago.

Vistas from the San Francisco Peaks reveal the hundreds of extinct volcanic cones and several lava domes that dot the southern edge of the Colorado Plateau. Inset: A ponderosa pine grows precariously on the side of the cinder cone known as Red Mountain.

overlying sediments were stripped away and the Redwall Limestone dissolved into a land of underground tunnels, caves, and sinkholes—a classic karst topography, so-called because of its resemblance to the Karst District of the Adriatic coast.

After a few million more years, the region was covered with another shallow sea where more gray limestone formed, interbedded with untold tons of reddish silt and sand washed in by rivers. The sea advanced and retreated numerous times, and the deposits grew to be hundreds of feet thick. Dissolved minerals in groundwater percolating through these sediments precipitated out and cemented the particles of silt and grains of sand into stone.

The lower five hundred feet of alternating beds of sandstone and siltstone are lumped together by geologists as the Supai Group. The narrow canyon or "inner gorge" of Oak Creek Canyon that begins near the mouth of Casner Canyon and runs downstream toward Sedona reveals Supai rocks.

Forming a steep slope above the Supai is two hundred feet of purplish red limey sandstone and siltstone called the Hermit Shale. Rivers flowing off the Ancestral Rockies carried sediments to their resting place here some 280 million years ago. Fossil impressions of fern fronds, worm trails, and footprints of small salamanderlike creatures are delicately preserved.

Over the next several million years, the Hermit floodplain gave way to a very salty, tidal flat situation which was then covered by wind-blown sands from the north. For millions and millions of years, grayish orange to reddish brown fine-grained sands were deposited in huge dunes. At one point, a shallow sea invaded and ten to thirty vertical feet of limestone (today classified as the Fort Apache Limestone) was laid down, followed by more eolian sand.

This eight hundred feet of wind-deposited sand eventually became the sandstone, the Schnebly Hill Formation, that forms the famous buttes and spires of the Red Rock Country, such as Coffee Pot Rock, Cathedral Rock, and Bell Rock.

Desert winds continued out of the north, eventually engulfing the area with buff-colored sand. Shifting sand dunes hundreds of feet thick collected for millions of years.

Fossil tracks of presumably small reptiles are common in this formation, the Coconino Sandstone. Angled lines marking cliff faces of the Coconino are crossbedded wind patterns frozen in time.

But the desert was not to last. By 250 million years ago, another sea was invading. The Kaibab ocean was full of life: mollusks, brachiopods, pelecypods, corals, trilobites, crinoids, gastropods including nautiloids, sponges, and early sharks. Calcium carbonate from shells and sand accumulated on the shallow sea floor to become the Kaibab Formation.

From Redwall time to the Kaibab Sea, the environment changed many times and, with these changes, life ebbed and flowed. Some plants and animals died out and new species evolved, but there were no mass extinctions. Then something very curious occurred at the end of the Paleozoic Era, some 225 million years ago.

Worldwide, one-half of the families of marine organisms, including trilobites, all ancient corals, all but one lineage of ammonites, and most bryozoans, brachiopods, and crinoids, died out in a few million years. This extinction was the most profound of several that occurred in the past 600 million years. The more well-known Cretaceous Period extinction of the dinosaurs ranks in second place, with a quarter of all families disappearing.

Dinosaurs were dramatic beasts, and their demise has caught the attention of geologists and laypeople alike. A cosmic intervention, in the form of an asteroid or meteor striking the earth and throwing a massive dust cloud into the atmosphere and changing the climate, is the leading contender as the cause of the dinosaurs' extinction.

The extinctions at the close of the Paleozoic Era, also known as the Permian die-off (the Permian Period is a subdivision of the Paleozoic Era), may be related to earthbound geologic events. Toward the end of the Permian, the continents, through the process of plate tectonics (commonly called continental drift), were bumping into each other and coalescing. The amount of shallow sea floor (continental shelf) adjacent to continents was drastically reduced as continental edges came together. Since most of the marine organisms were shallow-dwelling creatures, there simply was not enough room to support them all, resulting in wholesale extinctions.

ERAS: PALEOZOIC

Red Rock–Sacred Mountain Country Geologic Timeline	*about 330 million years ago:* Redwall Limestone ▲	*about 280 million years ago:* Hermit Shale ▲	*about 270 million years ago:* Coconino Sandstone ▲
	about 300 million years ago: Supai Group ▲	*about 275 million years ago:* Schnebly Hill Formation ▲	*about 250 million years ago:* Kaibab Formation ▲

Once the Kaibab Sea retreated, a period of erosion took place. Eventually northern Arizona and southern Utah returned to a hot, arid climate. Slow, meandering muddy rivers carried in more vermilion-colored sands and mud, which would ultimately become the Moenkopi Formation. In this rock layer are found reptile tracks left by pseudosuchians, the direct ancestors of the dinosaurs.

Later, the rivers began to carry in large rounded pebbles and sand from distant mountains. Besides sediments, an amazing number of evergreen logs were transported downstream and deposited. Over millions of years, the wood was slowly replaced with silica and other minerals to form rock replicas of the logs, called petrified wood. The colorful sediments along with their fossilized trees are the Chinle Formation, the same rock that makes up most of the Painted Desert to the north and east of Flagstaff.

Presumably many other sedimentary layers, perhaps ten thousand vertical feet worth, were stacked on top of this geologic layer cake as evidenced in the Mesozoic Age ("Dinosaur Age") rock units found to the north in southern Utah, but over the past 60 to 70 million years (the Cenozoic Age or "Age of Mammals") most have been stripped away by erosion as the Red Rock–Sacred Mountain area has been uplifted above sea level. Only bits and pieces of Moenkopi sandstone and shales are found in the immediate area.

Change is the only constant. On the geologic clock, oceans come and go; continents shift position, break apart, and rejoin; mountains are thrust up and eroded away; rivers run and dry up; dunes encroach and are buried— all in a geologic minute or two.

Fairly recently, geologically speaking, a few more rocks were added to our story; these are the lava flows, cinder deposits, and volcanoes that cap much of the Red Rock –Sacred Mountain area.

From outer space, astronauts have noted and photographed the splash of dark volcanic rock spread over northern-central Arizona that is the San Francisco Volcanic Field. Over six hundred volcanoes, primarily cinder cones, from the Little Colorado River west to Ash Fork and from Shadow Mountain near Cameron south to the Mogollon Rim have been counted as part of this extensive, three-thousand-square-mile volcanic field. The cinder cones range from barely detectable erosional remnants to steep, thousand-foot-high hills composed of reddish to black basaltic cinders. Explosive eruptions of frothy, gas-rich magma built up massive piles of cinders into cones. The cones and associated lava flows range in age from 8 million to a mere 740 years old (the red cinders along the crest of Sunset Crater were deposited about A.D. 1250).

The average span between eruptions has been roughly thirteen thousand years, but a more intriguing aspect regarding the timing is the fact that the younger eruptions occurred more frequently. These younger cones and flows are located generally to the northeast of the older ones. These facts led Dr. Harold Colton, founder of the Museum of Northern Arizona, to speculate that perhaps he would witness an eruption within his lifetime. Though Colton lived to be eighty-nine, the vulcan gods did not grant his wish. Today, most Flagstaff geologists are not too concerned about an imminent eruption. Still, you may want to avoid buying real estate northeast of Sunset Crater.

The earliest eruptions tended to be of basalt, a dark extrusive rock rich in iron minerals but low in silica. Basalt is the rock type that makes up the Hawaiian Islands. Good examples are exposed in various road cuts around Flagstaff and also at the head of Oak Creek Canyon. Where the lava cooled into smooth, billowy, ropy piles, the geologists refer to it with the Hawaiian term *pahoehoe*. Jagged flows, the result of the outer surface cooling while the magma underneath continued flowing and breaking the hardening surface is known as *aa*, which may be a reference to what one yells when trying to cross such a flow with bare feet.

When these eruptions ceased, molten lava within the flow sometimes continued to advance, draining corridors under the surface. These caves are known as lava tubes. Ironically, though the tubes are "born of fire," today they often hold ice well into summer. Back in 1915, west of the Peaks, lumbermen discovered Lava River Cave with its 3,600-foot-long tunnel. Local ranchers mined a large quantity of ice out of the tube.

Younger vents also spewed forth basalt, generally northeast of the older flows. By 2.5 million years ago, basalt flows had reached the valley of the Little Colorado River.

MESOZOIC ━━━━ CENOZOIC ━━━

about 225 million years ago: Permian die-off
▲

about 225 million years ago: Moenkopi Formation
▲

about 210 million years ago: Chinle Formation
▲

about 8 million to 740 years ago: lava flows and cinder deposits
▲

about 4 million years ago: andesites, dacites, and rhyolites that built up into lava domes
▲

Only during the spring runoff from the high country and after heavy rain showers does the Little Colorado River flow over Grand Falls, a 185-foot drop created when an ancient lava flow dammed the gorge previously carved by the river.

Why the composition of the lava changed through time is still an unanswered questioned.

Interspersed between these oldest and youngest basalt flows came a period, beginning about four million years ago, when a few new volcanic centers of different types of lava made their debut along major breaks or faults in the earth's crust. Out of these breaks light-colored, silica-rich lava spewed forth. These lavas were andesites, dacites, and rhyolites, all typically thick, viscous flows that formed thick, stubby flows and built up into steep-sided lava domes over their vents. Bill Williams Mountain (about 4 million years old), Sitgreaves Mountain (about 2.5 million years old), Kendrick Peak (about 3 million years old), and the considerably younger O'Leary Peak (about 200,000 years old) are examples.

Between 1.8 million and 400,000 years ago, the San Francisco Peaks were built up from alternating flows and cinders composed of primarily andesites and dacite. Eventually, a classic, cone-shaped composite or stratovolcano reaching to over fifteen thousand feet above sea level in elevation was formed. The lower west slope of the Peaks encompassing the area called Hart Prairie is a shield volcano, formed by successive flows of basalt. As the name implies, a shield volcano has a low vertical profile.

Near the southern and southeastern base of the Peaks, thick, pasty lavas piled up into the lava domes of the Dry Lake Hills and Mount Elden. The dacite of Mount Elden was so viscous that it often stopped flowing before reaching the bottom of the hill, and cooled into the rock lobes on the south and southwest slopes. These interesting shapes may have led to the Hopi name for the mountain, *Hovi'itstuyqa,* which translates as "buttocks sticking-out point."

The rising lava pushed up and overturned some of the underlying Paleozoic sedimentary rocks; this is especially evident on the northeast side of Elden where Devonian-age fossils of plated fish have been found. According to geologist Bill Breed, "To walk up the eastern slope of Mount Elden is thus like walking down the Kaibab Trail at Grand Canyon."

Very briefly, this summarizes where all these rocks came from. Now, how did all these rocks get shaped into today's landscape? In one word, erosion. Let's look at a few of the details.

On the San Francisco Peaks between 400,000 and 200,000 years ago, landslides, probably volcanically generated, decapitated the fifteen-thousand-foot mountain and sent debris mostly down the northeast slope toward Deadman Flat. Subsequent collapse formed the caldera of the ancestral Inner Basin which would later be subjected to glacial carving.

The past 200,000 years have seen at least three major periods of glaciation in North America. Although the incredibly huge continental glaciers never reached this far south, the colder temperatures associated with the glacial periods prevented winter snow from completely melting on the higher slopes of the Peaks. Over many winters, the accumulating snow became compacted into ice. Glaciers are not simply ice; they're ice and flowing water and vast amounts of rocky debris that scour, rasp, and pluck as gravity tugs.

The earliest glaciation (the Lockett Meadow Glaciation) of the Peaks occurred about 200,000 years ago. Glaciers over six hundred feet thick and up to four miles long flowed down Sugarloaf Mountain and probably down the north- and west-facing outer flanks of the Peaks. A warming period melted the ice, and plants slowly migrated upslope. After the warming period, a second glaciation took place (the Core Ridge Glaciation of the Early Wisconsinan Age, about 80,000 years ago and so named because the continental ice sheets reached what is now Wisconsin). At least seven glaciers coalesced in their descent through the Inner Basin to form a glacier over two miles long and about five hundred feet thick. Another warming period followed. A third glaciation developed (the Snowslide Spring Glaciation of Late Wisconsinan Age, about 11,000 years ago), producing only small glaciers in the cirques or bowl-shaped recesses beneath Humphreys, Agassiz, and Fremont peaks. Though temperatures were colder than during Core Ridge Glaciation time, lower snowfall amounts account for the smaller glaciers.

For the past ten thousand years, the Southwest has been thawing out and becoming more arid. For about three thousand years the climate rapidly warmed to conditions quite similar to those today. Then from about 7,000 to

CENOZOIC

about 1.8 million to 400,000 years ago: San Francisco Peaks built
▲

about 400,000 to 200,000 years ago: landslides on San Francisco peaks
▲

about 200,000 years ago: Lockett Meadow Glaciation
▲

about 80,000 years ago: Core Ridge Glaciation
▲

about 11,000 years ago: Snowslide Spring Glaciation
▲

Left: Long after thousands of feet of sandstone, shale, and limestone were deposited during the Paleozoic and Mesozoic eras, and then partially eroded during the Cenozoic, basalt flows capped the sedimentary layers. Above: As recently as 740 years ago, the volcanic cone Sunset Crater spewed out red cinders along its crest. Right: Worn, stream-tumbled boulders line the banks of Oak Creek.

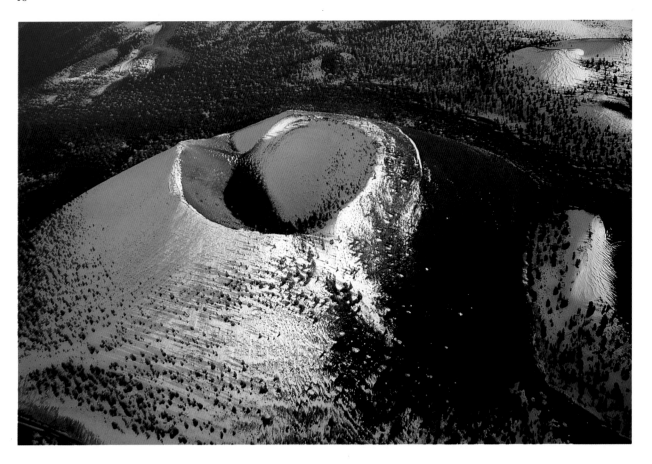

4,500 years ago, the Southwest was distinctly warmer than it is at present and suffered from long periods of drought. For the past 4,500 years, the climate has been moderately warm and extended droughts occurred in 500 B.C., A.D. 330, 1276–1299, and 1573–1593.

Besides the constant wearing down of the volcanic mountains, uplift and erosion have been at work on the underlying sedimentary rocks for the past sixty to seventy million years. The Mogollon Rim to the south is the erosional scar of land faulted and retreating at the hand of erosion. Canyons like Oak Creek, Sycamore, and Walnut reveal more earth movements accompanied by the downcutting of running water and widening primarily by freeze-thaw action; that is, by moisture seeping into cracks, freezing (thus expanding), and breaking the rock apart. Gravity and running water take over from there, transporting the pieces ever closer to the sea. The earth is hardly at peace; it is amazingly dynamic. But in our lifetime we rarely glimpse more than a frame or two of the very, very long geologic movie.

I run my hand over the rough edge of a volcanic boulder. This rock is not unlike the igneous extrusions found on the moon's surface except that here on earth the rock will be etched by acids released by lichens and weathered by rain and wind into gravel and then into finer particles of sand, silt, and clay, mixed with organic litter to become soil, warmed by the sun, watered by the summer rains and winter snows, to become the substrate for the tenacious grip of life.

It's now late morning. The thermals have lifted moisture-laden air high into the stratosphere. Mountains of cumulus soar thirty thousand feet into the intense cobalt blue sky. I examine some small, glassy patches on the volcanic rock – fulgurites – that have been formed by lightning strikes melting the stone. Distant thunder warns me that the time has come to make a hasty retreat down the mountain.

As I approach the safety of the Snow Bowl Lodge, the thunderstorm explodes with a fury. Here is erosion in action. Tiny rivulets quickly form, which in turn join into streams, which merge into larger streams and finally into torrents of rushing energy. A valley is cut deeper; another canyon begins.

Later this afternoon, the cooling rains and the coming of night lower the temperature and dissipate the storm. Under a bejeweled night sky, the warm rocks will quickly lose their heat energy to the infinite heat sink of space. And somewhere, high on the mountain, water in the cracks of the rocks will freeze, expand, and split its host. This is geology in action, repetitious, dramatic or subtle, but definitely timeless and methodical.

Above: Sunset Crater is the most recent cinder cone of over six hundred located on the San Francisco volcanic field. Sunset first came to life during the winter of 1064–65 and erupted periodically for nearly two hundred years. Below left: The massive tan Coconino Sandstone cliffs exposed in Oak Creek Canyon are essentially petrified sand dunes from a desert that covered northern Arizona about 270 million years ago. Generally, the Coconino sandstone forms vertical cliffs, but erosion occasionally produces fanciful shapes. Below right: Rain water caught in natural depressions in the rock serves as an important water source for wildlife including certain amphibians and invertebrates.

PEOPLE
WITHOUT WATER

SERENDIPITY. UNEXPECTED DISCOVERIES ARE often just that – fortunate accidents. And so it was on a hot, muggy afternoon in late July 1991. Peter Pilles, forest archaeologist for the Coconino National Forest, found himself tackling a steep, brushy slope in an attempt to reach a small cave. Just days before, passengers aboard a helicopter flight out of Sedona had reported seeing several large prehistoric pots sitting in a cave above a small ruin. One of the passengers was Andy Seagle. Upon returning to Sedona, he called the forest archaeologist to report the discovery. He excitedly told Pilles about the find and how his interest in early cultures had been spurred by an older brother, a budding archaeologist. This brother had tragically died of cystic fibrosis, was cremated, and was then buried in the Red Rock Country.

Pilles cautiously asked, "Was your brother's name Tim?"

Incredulous, Seagle replied, "Why, yes. How did you know?" Pilles explained that years before, Tim Seagle had worked with him at the Museum of Northern Arizona in Flagstaff. Before ending their phone conversation, the two men decided that it would be fitting to name the cave in Tim's memory.

As Pilles scrambled upward, he could feel his heart pounding. Was it just from the exertion of the climb or from the anticipation of what he might find in Tim's Cave?

At last, he reached the final cliff leading to the cave. A tall ladder was put in place and he began his ascent. There sat three whole pots, part of a fourth, and four baskets, presumably just as they had been placed by the

Sinagua over seven centuries ago. This was an archaeologist's dream come true: to see whole pots *in situ,* unmolested through time, and associated with a group of dwellings.

Pilles photographed each artifact in place and meticulously took notes and measurements. His primary concern was to not disturb the site until a detailed survey could be done. He also worried about the artifacts' safety.

Who were these ancient people who had so carefully cached these pots and baskets?

Basically, they were farmers—farmers living on the edge, unfamiliar with the deep, fertile, well-watered loams of the Midwest. These farmers scratched out tiny plots in the rock-, sand-, and clay-based, nutrient-poor soils often dry as dust. By A.D. 700, these agrarian folks living in the Red Rock–Sacred Mountain area were culturally distinctive enough to warrant future archaeologists' attention and classification. In the 1930s, Dr. Harold S. Colton, founder of the Museum of Northern Arizona, borrowed the old Spanish name for the waterless mountains around Flagstaff—*Sierra de Sin Agua*—and applied it to this prehistoric culture.

Geographically, the Sinagua can be divided into two populations: those who lived in the Verde Valley and the drainages flowing off the Mogollon Rim, a thousand-foot or more escarpment that abruptly separates the Colorado Plateau from Arizona's central mountains and valleys, and a northern group that lived above the Rim near the San Francisco Peaks. The farmers in the Verde had to deal with long, hot summers; their northern neighbors enjoyed cooler temperatures but a shorter growing season followed by snowy winters.

The early Southern Sinagua, who date back to about A.D. 700, lived in shallow, rectangular pithouses, structures built partly below the surface of the ground. Posts supported a roof, and other poles, brush, and clay finished off the side walls. The Sinagua did not excel at pottery making; theirs was a plain reddish brown ware used primarily for cooking. Decorated pottery was imported from the Kayenta Anasazi, who lived to the north along the Little Colorado River and beyond. The secrets of agriculture apparently were brought by the Hohokam farmers of central and southern Arizona who moved in with or adjacent to the Sinagua.

Soon the people were dry-farming mesa tops and irrigating fields along streams. The mesa tops had a longer growing season than the valleys, where heavy, dense cold air often settled. Also, the mesa tops received more sunshine, and there is evidence that some farm plots were placed near large boulders to take advantage of radiant

heat. The cultivated corn was ground into meal using large, rectangular manos and trough-shaped metates. The corn, beans, and squash added to the Sinagua's diet of gathered wild edibles and wild meat.

Over the next several centuries, the Sinagua population increased, resulting in larger pithouses, usually round instead of rectangular and much deeper than in the past. A few people began to live in two- and three-room pueblos. Walled-in, oval ballcourts (whose exact use is unknown but possibly was similar to that of the prehistoric ballcourts built by Aztecs and Mayans in Mexico) and stylized platform mounds were constructed, presumably for ceremonial use. They resembled similar structures built by the Hohokam people.

Above the Mogollon Rim, in the cooler, wetter climate of the high country, the early Northern Sinagua also lived in pithouses. The pithouses came in many styles—circular or squarish, with four to six posts supporting the roof and a lateral entry or antechamber. Their homes were sometimes clumped into villages of ten or more and were concentrated east of the Peaks around Turkey Tanks, Cinder Park, and to the southeast along the east base of Anderson Mesa. An occasional large subterranean room up to twenty-eight feet in diameter and five feet deep was built, presumably for community gatherings like the Great Kivas of the Anasazi.

Permanent streams and rivers are nonexistent in the Peaks area, so all farming relied upon precipitation. The farmers planted their crops and prayed that enough rain would fall. Often fields were strategically placed so they would be flooded by storm runoff. Corn and beans were raised in the larger parks or open meadows; small plots of edible wild plants were planted along washes. Most of the villages were set up in the transition zone between the ponderosa pine forest and the warmer but drier pinyon-juniper woodland. A tenuous balance existed: The crops had to be low enough in elevation to have a long, frost-free growing season yet high enough to receive an adequate supply of rain. Deer, bighorn sheep, and other game were an importance food resource. Wild plant foods also added to the larder.

About A.D. 900 a string of drier and warmer years caused much of the population to shift to the larger and presumably more dependable springs along the lower flanks of the San Francisco Peaks and Mount Elden. Communities on Anderson Mesa stayed in place, but both groups built additional check dams to catch any runoff and channel it to their fields.

The farming life in this agriculturally marginal land was difficult but sustainable. And unlike their feudal European

The Northern Sinagua pueblo known as Wukoki seems to grow straight out of a pedestal of Moenkopi Sandstone. Wukoki's inhabitants had a commanding view of the Painted Desert and the San Francisco Peaks.

Left: Between A.D. 1000 and 1130, the Southern Sinagua of the Red Rock Country consolidated into villages. The cliff house of Palatki typifies this period. Above: Wupatki National Monument, northeast of Flagstaff, contains more than two thousand archaeological sites. These sites are the remains of three separate and distinct cultures—the Kayenta Anasazi, the Sinagua, and the Cohonina—who lived in the area about eight hundred years ago.

counterparts, the Sinagua lived as free people working cooperatively. Soon, however, a series of natural events would dramatically and irrevocably impact the Sinagua's lives.

During the fall of 1064, as the people were finishing harvesting their corn and beans and carefully drying these precious goods for the long winter ahead, the earth began to tremble and moan a few miles east of the San Francisco Peaks in Bonito Park.

Why was Mother Earth so restless? Were the gods angry? Most if not all of the residents in the immediate area packed up their belongings and moved to quieter ground. In some cases, the roof beams and support posts of their pithouses were also removed, suggesting that the quaking earth gave ample warning.

This exodus was unknown to archaeologists until 1930, when a geologist from the Museum of Northern Arizona, Major Lionel F. Brady, was asked to take a visiting artist to Sunset Crater, a dramatic volcanic cinder cone (and today a national monument) northeast of Flagstaff. A good vantage point was from a large meadow known as Bonito Park. There the artist began to paint. Brady wandered about the field and found a few old potsherds, which he shoved into his pocket and later showed to museum director Dr. Colton.

Colton's curiosity was piqued, and a crew was sent to dig a test-trench in Bonito Park. After digging down through a thick layer of volcanic ash, the archaeologists and geologist were amazed to discover a pithouse. People had been living here before and possibly during the volcano's eruption. Sunset Crater was much younger than was formerly thought. Serendipity at work.

Sometime during the winter of 1064–65, the ground cracked open and volcanic cinders and ash began to explode violently from the earth. By summer, the dark brown cinder cone was one thousand feet high and a black lava flow had spilled forth from its eastern base. All the trees, shrubs, and grasses within a two-mile radius around the volcano were dead from fire, poisonous gases, or acidic rains, or were buried under a heavy blanket of ash. Plant life up to fifteen miles away was affected.

For nearly two centuries the volcano sporadically erupted, sending out more ash, cinders, and lava bombs.

Eventually one-half billion tons of mostly jet black cinders covered eight hundred square miles. Prevailing winds may have blown ash as far east as Kansas. The jagged Bonito Lava Flow emerged out of the western base of Sunset Crater in 1180. During its last breath about 1250, the volcano coughed out the red cinders that line the crest, giving the summit ridge of mountain a perpetual "sunset glow," which led geologist and Colorado River explorer John Wesley Powell to bestow the name Sunset Peak in 1892.

An apparent increase in the number of pithouses and pueblos after the eruption led early archaeologists to suggest that the deposition of volcanic ash initiated a land rush of sorts with the immigration of Anasazi, Mogollon, Hohokam, and other prehistoric cultures. It was thought that the volcanic ash acted as a mulch and contributed soil nutrients, which improved farming. Also, the appearance of artifacts representative of previously distant cultures presumably meant those people had arrived in the Flagstaff area. However, more recent studies have shown that this particular ash has little nutrient value to offer plants. Today's archaeologists, such as Peter Pilles, have an alternative explanation for the number of sites before and after the Sunset Crater eruption.

A few years prior to the eruption, a subtle change in the area's climate began to occur. From about 1050 to 1130, the annual rainfall and annual average temperature increased slightly, which in this semi-arid region can significantly encourage plant growth. The evidence for this climatic shift is found in the annual growth rings of trees. The tree rings dating from this period are noticeably wider than earlier and later ones. Serendipity at work, again.

Although the volcanic ash can act as a mulch and slow evaporation of the increased moisture, the increase in precipitation probably played a far greater role in attracting farmers. A light cover of dark ash absorbs heat, which can "lengthen" the growing season, a critical factor at high elevations.

The apparent increase in population in the Sunset Crater area turned out to be illusionary; populations simply were redistributed. As more archaeological surveys have been done outside the ash-fall area, equally dense populations have been discovered. Additionally, what seemed to be increased migration has been explained as the result of increased trade between the Sinagua and their neighbors. The Sinagua were not an isolated island of culture in the shadow of a volcano. At that time, trade items commonly traveled as far as from southern Mexico to central Utah. Shells from the Pacific, copper bells manufactured in Mexico, macaw parrot feathers from the tropics, and turquoise from New Mexico hint at the extent of the early trade routes. Important export items were obsidian, mined primarily from Government Mountain, and salt dug from a deposit in the Verde Valley.

The Northern Sinagua discovered that they could now raise crops at lower elevations, at the desert's edge to the north and east of the Peaks, though sites close to the mountain such as the Mount Elden pueblo remained important. Many of the spectacular pueblos in Wupatki National Monument and cliff dwellings in Walnut Canyon were constructed at this time. The Sinagua at Wupatki were now closer to their Kayenta Anasazi neighbors, who were building Lomaki and Crack-in-the-Rock pueblos.

Between A.D. 1000 and 1130, the Southern Sinagua consolidated into villages. Small, several-roomed pueblos combined to form some forty larger pueblos and cliff houses along the Verde River and its sidestreams, although the uplands were not totally abandoned. The large cliff houses known as Honanki near Loy Butte and Palatki in Red Canyon, with intermediate numbers of rooms and larger communal rooms, typify this period. During the following two centuries, great hilltop pueblos, such as the one-hundred-room Tuzigoot and the grand, five-story cliff dwelling called Montezuma's Castle, reached their zenith.

Though toiling in the fields and hunting and gathering must have taken the bulk of their time, the Sinagua reserved some time for pageantry. East of Flagstaff, at a site known as Ridge Ruin, a burial was excavated of a man wearing shell and turquoise ear pendants, a nose plug of dark red argillite with buttons of turquoise at either end, and a skull cap. With him were buried over six hundred artifacts including pottery, baskets, arrowheads, other jewelry, pouches filled with mineral paints, and twelve wooden wands—each tipped with an ornamental head.

These wands may link him to a rite, similar to the magic trick of sword-swallowing, in which a priest "swallows" the stick while under the protection of the beast symbolized on the stick's head.

The timing varies a little from place to place, but at least by the early 1450s, both the northern and southern Sinagua seemed to have abandoned the region. Why did they leave? Drought, disease, and over-use of the natural resources are all possibilities, and the question is still debated.

Where did they go? The popular theory is that they merged with the Hopi, perhaps in stages, first at Nuvakwewtaqa in Chavez Pass and then at the Homolovi villages near Winslow and eventually to the Hopi Mesas. One problem with this idea, however, is that some archaeologists claim that other groups, notably the Anasazi, merged with the Hopi. The sizes of these early Hopi villages do not suggest the huge populations necessary to account for this merging of various cultures. While there is little doubt of cultural and historical ties between the Hopi and Sinagua, much still needs to be learned about the Sinagua's fate.

Archaeologists know a great deal about the early farmers because of their abundant ruins and artifacts, but people lived in the Red Rock–Sacred Mountain area long before the Sinagua. Artifacts of these earlier people date back about four thousand years. Archaeologists have labeled these folks the Archaic Culture (more specifically for this area, the Dry Creek Phase of the Archaic Culture), a loosely associated group of hunters and gatherers that traveled through the intermountain west including the Colorado Plateau from about 6500 B.C. to about the birth of Christ. They may have lived in the Red Rock–Sacred Mountain area for centuries, but only a few clues suggest their presence.

In the Dry Creek area, Archaic stone artifacts such as points and small basin-shaped grinding stones, which are indicative of pulverizing seeds and nuts, have been found. In Sycamore and Walnut canyons, a few animal-shaped figurines fashioned out of split twigs have been recovered and radiocarbon dated at between three thousand and four thousand years old. And several ghostlike pictographs similar to the Archaic Barrier Canyon–style found in Utah and the Grand Canyon are known in the Red Rock Country.

continued on page 38

Prior to the Archaic, an earlier group known as the Paleo-Indians, or Lithic Cultural Stage, may have hunted here for remnant herds of Ice Age mammals such as mammoth, shrub oxen, bison, sloths, camels, and horses, but no definitive sites have yet been located in the Verde Valley or near Flagstaff. The closest locations for Paleo-Indian artifacts are stone points found at Wupatki National Monument and Winslow.

After the Archaic Period and following the Sinagua, other people were drawn to the area. A hunting-gathering people wearing "crowns of painted sticks on their heads and jicaras [small bowls] of mescal and pinyon nuts and bread made from it" were encountered in the Verde Valley in May 1583 by the Spaniard Antonio de Espejo. Fifteen years later, Marcos Farfán de los Godos explored the Verde Valley and named the residents "Cruzados," a reference to the small wooden crosses they wore on their heads. This headdressing, incidentally, led the Spaniards to falsely conclude that the natives were Christians.

The "Cruzados," who called themselves *Wipukpaya* – "people at the foot of the mountains" – regarded the Red Rock Country as their ancestral and spiritual home. (At one time, some anthropologists suspected that the farming Sinagua returned to a hunting and gathering lifeway at the end of the fourteenth century and evolved into the Wipukpaya, one of the four subgroups of the Yavapai; this theory is now fairly well discounted.)

Wipukpaya legend recalls:

"From the underworld, all humans and animals ascended on the first maize plant. The hole through which they came then filled with water and today is called Montezuma's Well. After the second world was destroyed by fire, the third world was destroyed by flood. One person, Kamalapukwia, survived inside a hollow agave stalk that settled in Boynton Canyon as the flood waters subsided. She lived in a cave and soon became impregnated by Sun and Cloud and gave birth to a daughter, who in turn bore a son, Lofty Wanderer. He called all the creatures of the world together in a cave in Hartwell Canyon and taught each their right ways and then sent the different races of man to the far corners of the world. The Wipukpaya alone stayed at the Center of the World where everything had begun."

The Wipukpaya still speak of the "little people" who inhabit the red rocks. They are said to be about three feet tall, have round heads, eyes and a mouth, but no nose. They wear skirts of fresh juniper twigs and can appear as a whirlwind or be heard hollering in the canyons.

The early "people at the foot of the mountains" lived in caves or pole-domed huts thatched with grass. The base of the hut may have been bermed with dirt and the top waterproofed with animal skins. Shades, or ramadas, were often used during the hot summer.

As time passed, the Wipukpaya began to plant a little corn, beans, squash, and tobacco in moist areas such as Indian Gardens and in the West Fork of Oak Creek Canyon, but primarily they continued to hunt game and gather wild plant foods. Their greatest food supply was harvested in the fall when acorns, pinyon nuts, Arizona black walnuts, sunflower seeds, goldeneye seeds, wild grasses, manzanita berries, juniper berries, hackberries, squawberries, wild grapes, cactus fruits, mesquite beans, and the fruit of the banana yucca were ripe. The agave, or century plant, was an important year-round food source. It was dug up, the leaves cut off, and the "heart" roasted in a pit for several days. The cooked, squashlike interior was then eaten or dried and stored for future use. Wipukpaya families may have spent three to four months in one area gathering and preparing agaves.

Sadly, in a pattern repeated throughout North America during the nineteenth century, the Indian presence could not be tolerated by the ever-increasing Anglo-pioneer population. Over six hundred Indians were settled on a reservation along the Verde River, but others resisted. General George Crook arrived in the Verde Valley to quell raiding by Yavapai-Apache (by this time members of the Tonto Apache, a group of people from east-central Arizona, had intermingled with the Yavapai). Crook was a striking figure – over six feet tall, adorned with reddish "burnside" whiskers, and usually dressed unconventionally in canvas hunting clothes. He allowed his men a similar casual dress.

In November of 1872, he began his offensive. His tactic was to keep the "hostiles" moving, to wear them out and exhaust their food supply. Six months later, in April, the Yavapai-Apache renegade leaders Chalipun and Delshay surrendered.

Crook was equally effective in convincing the Yavapai-Apache that reservation life in the Verde Valley could not only be tolerated but profitable through the sale of surplus crops. Unfortunately, some ambitious, influential ranchers and unscrupulous government officials succeeded in having the Rio Verde Reservation abolished and the land opened to non-Indian settlement.

About 1,400 Yavapai-Apache were forced to march to the San Carlos Reservation in east-central Arizona during the winter of 1875. Nearly one hundred people died en route. Not until the 1890s did some of the Yavapai-Apache receive permission to return to the Verde Valley. Another twenty years would pass before an official

Previous pages: The grand, five-story cliff dwelling called Montezuma Castle reached its largest size by the 1300s and was occupied for another century before being abandoned. Above: Shortly after the winter solstice, the Hopi kachinas (spirits), leave Nuvatukya'ovi (San Francisco Peaks) and travel to the Hopi Mesas. Kachinas intercede with the forces of nature to promote life by bringing rain to the arid land.

30

Above: According to the Wipukpaya (Yavapai), all humans and animals ascended into this world from the underworld through a hole that was later filled with water. Montezuma's Well, a natural spring within a collapsed cavern near the Red Rock Country, supposedly is the place of emergence. Left: Although the Sinagua grew corn, beans, and squash, game animals and wild plant foods added to their larder.

reservation would be set up for their exclusive use. Today, the descendants of the Wipukpaya live on the Camp Verde, Middle Verde, and Clarkdale reservations.

Far to the northeast of the Wipukpaya are the Hopi, pueblo-dwelling people who, like the Sinagua, are dry-farmers. Some Hopi clans trace their ancestry to the "place of the red rocks," a warm, well-watered land to the south – the Red Rock Country perhaps? A link with the southern Sinagua? Archaeologists wonder.

From their mesa-top villages, the Hopi look out across the stark Painted Desert toward the lofty *Nuvatukya'ovi,* "the place of snow on the very top." In 1629, Franciscan missionaries established several missions and "visitas" among the Hopi and christened the distant but imposing mountain the Sierra de San Francisco after the founder of their order. Uttering the traditional Hopi name was forbidden.

The missionaries didn't appreciate the deep, reverent connection the Hopi have to the Peaks. According to legend, shortly after the winter solstice the kachinas, who are ancestor spirits as well as animal and plant spirits, come from *Nuvatukya'ovi* to the mesas to hear the prayers of the Hopi and carry them to the gods. Kachinas can also intercede with the forces of nature to promote life, most commonly in bringing rain to the Hopi mesas. Without the life-giving summer rains, the Hopi would perish and blow away with the next sandstorm. By mid-July the prayers for rain are answered in the form of thunderstorms that seem to be born on the summit of the Peaks and race out across the desert to the mesas. Their mission accomplished, the Kachinas return to the spirit world via the mountain.

Like the Hopi, the Navajo also venerate the San Francisco Peaks. The Navajo have been here forever in spirit, but only recently in body. Legend relates how some Navajo sought refuge in the Red Rock Country to escape Kit Carson's 1863–1864 federally sanctioned campaign to remove the Navajo to a prisoner camp, Bosque Redondo, in New Mexico.

Like that of the Yavapai, Apache, and Hopi, the Navajo's traditional oral history speaks of previous worlds destroyed and new ones created with emergence into this current existence between the four sacred mountains: Mount Taylor in New Mexico, Hesperus and Blanca peaks in Colorado, and the San Francisco Peaks. The Navajo call the Arizona sacred mountain *Do'ko'oslid,* which means "blue western mountain" or "abalone shell mountain," marking not only the *geographical* perimeter of their world but also the boundaries of their world of order and stability.

Left: The metate and mano were used primarily to grind corn, the staple of the ancient Sinagua. Above: South-facing Sinagua cliff houses in Walnut Canyon catch the winter sun but are partially shaded during the summer when the sun is higher in the sky. Right: What happened to the Sinagua? Some archaeologists believe that they merged with the Hopi, perhaps in stages, first at Nuvakwewtaqa in Chavez Pass and then at the Homolovi villages near Winslow and finally to the Hopi Mesas. The meaning of these Sinagua petroglyphs near Chavez Pass is lost in time.

At a hearing concerning the sacredness of the San Francisco Peaks, Navajo Frank Goldtooth, Jr., related:

"This peak was made by the holy people in the beginning. At that time when it was made only by the holy people, not by the white people nor any Indians, it was made just by the holy people and this thing here, this San Francisco Peak is prayers, is a prayer and it is sitting there with prayers and it has white shell beads and turquoise and Apache tear drops and abalone and that is what is sitting there with also plants of life, sitting there with life."

Staid anthropologists insist the Navajo are Athapaskan in origin and migrated down through the Great Plains hunting the bison and elk. According to these scientists, the Navajo did not arrive in Arizona until about 1700, over one hundred years after the first Spaniards.

All these native peoples have been and continue to be aligned with the earth. Their past, present, and future are irrevocably governed by the land – a land that they do not perceive as personal property but cherish as custodians. There is a Navajo prayer: *Nahasdzaan ts'ida biya nishli* – "I am truly, absolutely, without a doubt, a child of the Earth."

Anthropologists and archaeologists continue to study and try to understand the long human involvement with the Red Rock–Sacred Mountain region. To piece this story together, especially the prehistory, scientists must rely on the few artifacts left behind by the former residents. Unfortunately, archaeological artifacts have also caught the eye of the unauthorized collector and witless vandal.

Back in the Forest Service's archaeological office in Flagstaff, the euphoria over the discovery of Tim's Cave wasn't to last. Before Pilles and his staff had an opportunity to study the artifacts in detail and decide their fate, someone stole four of them: one redware jar, one yucca sifter basket, and two coiled baskets. The remaining artifacts were retrieved and placed under tight security. On the black market, the stolen pieces may sell for several hundred dollars, but their scientific value is priceless. Studying the minerals in the clay pots and comparing the results with known mineral and clay sources can reveal trade routes. An exciting new technique that involves rinsing out the inside of the pot and searching for traces of the genetic material DNA may tell what was cooked or stored in it. The archaeologists' dream find has turned into their worst nightmare.

Perhaps serendipity and science will solve the crime.

Lomaki, one of the ruins within Wupatki National Monument, is believed to have been built by Kayenta Anasazi, close neighbors to the Northern Sinagua.

EXPLORERS AND SCIENTISTS

AUTUMN IS A WONDERFUL time to be in Arizona's High Country—warm, bright days followed by crisp, clear nights. But the Spaniards who explored this territory in the sixteenth century cared little for its beauty. Gold and silver were foremost on their minds. In all their existing trip journals, no mention is made of the San Francisco Peaks that dominated the horizon.

Francisco Vázquez de Coronado, accompanied by 225 mounted men, sixty-two foot soldiers, fifty civilians of mixed ethnic backgrounds, and about seven hundred friendly Indians and Indian servants, had set out in 1540 in search of the fabled Seven Cities of Cibola. An earlier report had described houses two and three stories high and rich in turquoise. Surely there were other hidden treasures. Coronado's entourage trekked north out of old

Mexico, passed through the White Mountains of eastern Arizona, and after four grueling months discovered, much to their dismay, that the riches of Cibola were nothing more than the modest adobe villages of the Zuni people. While he continued his quest for gold northeasterly into the Great Plains of present-day Kansas, Coronado sent out a small exploratory party led by Pedro de Tovar to investigate tales of other villages to the west of Zuni.

After a month, Tovar returned to Cibola with the disappointing news that though he had encountered more pueblos, they, too, were composed only of adobe and rock houses—these were the Hopi villages. However, the Hopi had told him of a great river farther west and a land inhabited by large bodied people (presumably Havasupai, denizens of the Grand Canyon, who are generally taller and heavier than Hopi). So at the end of August, Coronado dispatched García López de Cárdenas to find the river. In late September, Cárdenas and his band of soldiers became the first Europeans to see the Grand Canyon and the Colorado River from the rim. Again, neither the scenery nor the native people impressed them.

After three days of trying to descend into the canyon's depths, the party made their way back to Cibola via the Hopi villages. Eventually all the Spaniards and their companions went home.

Four decades later, Antonio de Espejo, a prosperous rancher and merchant from southern Chihuahua, Mexico, left his home ostensibly to rescue two Franciscan priests being held captive by Indians near today's Socorro, New Mexico. He was also spurred along on his journey by pending murder charges, having been accused of killing one of his ranch foremen. Once in New Mexico, he learned that the priests had been killed. The resourceful Espejo decided to spend some time searching for valuable minerals. Natives near Santa Fe claimed that a rich deposit was located far to the west. At Zuni, he was excited to hear more about the alleged mines. Again, at Hopi, he heard more tales of rich mines, so in the spring of 1583, Espejo acquired Hopi guides and headed south to became the first European to penetrate the Red Rock–Sacred Mountain area.

Espejo and four other Spaniards apparently were led along an ancient trail, dubbed the Palatkwapi Trail by Northern Arizona University Professor James W. Byrkit, who has extensively studied this old route and has brought to light its historical significance. The name he chose is a Hopi place-name that refers to a "place of the red rocks," which may be the Sedona area.

The trail winds from the Hopi mesas to the Verde Valley via Chavez Pass (also spelled Chaves), then around the marshes known today as Long and Soldier lakes, past Pine Springs, and off the Mogollon Rim into the Verde Valley via Stoneman Lake and Rattlesnake Canyon to Beaverhead Springs.

The expedition's chronicler, Diego Pérez de Luxan, noted ". . . an abundance of grapevines and . . . many walnut and other trees. This is a warm land in which there are parrots." The Arizona black walnuts and wild grapes still exist, but the reference to parrots has long intrigued ornithologists. One possibility is that the local people had acquired parrots from Mexico through trade. Macaw feathers have been found in Sinagua and Anasazi sites. Alternatively, ornithologist Amadeo Rea believes it is possible that the Verde Valley area was within the historical range of the Carolina parakeet. Another possibility is that

the birds were native thick-billed parrots. In 1987, thick-billed parrots were released in the Chiricahua Mountains of southeastern Arizona, an area that is known to have been historic habitat for the birds. Within a year, eight of the eleven released parrots had flown over two hundred miles to Tonto Creek, which drains off of the Mogollon Rim not far from the Red Rock Country. The parrots were observed feeding on ponderosa pine seeds and casting the cones to the ground.

Luxan reported that one of Espejo's mules was "dashed to pieces" while descending a steep section of trail. The path forked at Beaverhead Springs: One branch went south to a salt mine (the sodium chloride was deposited two to six million years ago when subsidence of the Verde Valley floor caused the Verde River to become impounded); the other trail headed west crossing Oak Creek and the Verde River to the copper deposit on the slopes of Mingus Mountain that three centuries later would give rise to the fabulous mining town of Jerome. Although Espejo's official report enthusiastically proclaimed that the ". . . ores . . . are very rich and contain a great deal of silver," Luxan wrote, ". . . the mines were so worthless that we did not find in any of them a trace of silver, as they were copper mines, and poor." The Spaniards returned to their home in Mexico by September.

Fifteen years later, in 1598, the first governor of New Mexico sent Marcos Farfán de los Godos and eight companions to explore Arizona and, not coincidentally, to investigate the mines of the Verde Valley. He no doubt traveled the same route as Espejo, except that it was winter and the high country was blanketed with snow. Near Hay Lake, they encountered many "Jumanas" Indians (most likely Yavapai) who offered them powdered ores, some pieces of venison, and a tray of ground dates—a fascinating observance because the nearest native palms known today are located in the Kofa Mountains of southwestern Arizona. Another translation of this account says the tray contained fruit of the datil, or yucca. The large, pulpy yucca fruits were eaten raw or roasted and were a main staple of the Yavapai diet.

Farfán and his men marched off the snow-covered rim down into the Verde Valley, where they saw good pastures and abundant "deer, hares, and partridges (quail)." Two days later they arrived at the mines and staked about seventy mineral claims. In 1605, New Mexico's Governor Oñate visited the mines and was probably the last Spaniard to travel the Palatkwapi Trail.

The records of Espejo and Farfán leave much to speculation, but they both refer to the Sierra de Sin Agua, which may have been the San Francisco Peaks. Scant

Sunset illuminates an aspen grove on the edge of Hart Prairie.

reference is made to the red rock cliffs and buttes that they undoubtedly would have seen from many points along the trail. Philosophical historians have suggested that Europeans, in this case the Spaniards, were unprepared at this early time to appreciate wild nature and scenery. Untamed wilderness was to be dealt with as best as one could without forgetting the true objectives of the exploration – fortune, power, and saving "heathen" souls.

Not until the beginning of the nineteenth century did the first Americans of northern European descent enter the region; these were trappers such as Antoine Leroux, Bill Williams, and James Ohio Pattie. By mid-century, the United States government became interested in this territory and initiated a series of surveys for potential wagon roads and railroads.

In 1851, the first government survey was captained by Lorenzo Sitgreaves. His primary objective was to lay out a route across northern Arizona between New Mexico and the Pacific coast. Wisely, Sitgreaves chose the knowledgeable mountain man Leroux as his guide. Additionally, Sitgreaves brought along the first European scientists to study the indigenous flora and fauna, most notably Samuel Woodhouse, who also served as the expedition's physician. Woodhouse not only collected many plants and ten animals new to science but left a remarkable firsthand account of surviving a rattlesnake bite. He had been bitten while in the Zuni country and, as a good naturalist and doctor, kept detailed notes of his ordeal.

Two years later, a second survey team, this one led by Lieutenant Amiel Weeks Whipple, passed by the foot of the San Francisco Peaks. Accompanying Whipple was the French geologist Jules Marcou, who had come to the United States with the eminent naturalist Jean Louis Rodolphe Agassiz. As a member of this expedition, Marcou became the first geologist to cross the American continent.

Also with Whipple were zoologist C. B. R. Kennerly, a physician/botanist by the name of Dr. J. M. Bigelow, and a topographer/artist and self-described naturalist, Baldwin Mollhausen.

The beauty of the area made a powerful impression on the men, as noted by Mollhausen while the party was camped at Turkey Tanks on Christmas Day: ". . . we looked up at the sublime summits of the San Francisco Mountains, and needed no temple made with hands wherein to worship our Creator."

Unfortunately (from a naturalist's point of view), the expedition traversed the Sacred Mountain area in the dead of winter. However, Kennerly did observe:

"A few short marches through the dark pine forest and deep snow brought us near Mount Sitgreaves, which lay like a huge monster wrapped in the unspotted mantle of winter, while from its base stretched beautiful valleys covered with grass and dotted by clumps of cedars. Ascending the mountain, we found it the deserted home of the grizzly bear, which, chilled by the drifting snow that had also buried his food, had passed towards the south in search of more comfortable quarters. The number of trails of this animal that we found here, all leading towards the south, is almost incredible. Indeed, before the falling of the snow, it seemed to have been the peculiar home of this animal. But now he is gone, leaving the tufted squirrel and wolf the sole proprietors of his former domain."

In 1857, a very unusual survey team crossed northern Arizona. Lieutenant Edward F. Beale and his men, many of them Greeks and Turks in native dress, traveled with twenty-five camels to assess the animals' usefulness in the arid Southwest. Although the experiment was deemed a success, the outbreak of the Civil War several years later interrupted further camel caravans.

Beale returned in 1858 and 1859 to complete a wagon road across northern Arizona. He prophetically proclaimed, "This will eventually be the greatest emigrant road to California." The Beale Road, of course, eventually became the famous Route 66.

While building the wagon road, Beale extolled the virtues of the high country surrounding the Sacred Mountain: "The weather is delightful; no one could pass through this country without being struck with its picturesque and beautiful scenery, its rich soil, and noble forests of timber; the soil is rich black loam, the grass grama and bunch equally mixed, and the timber, pine of the finest quality, and greatest size; water at this season [April] we find everywhere, nor is there at any time any lack of it at this place [Leroux Springs]."

Surveyors, escorted by General William Jackson

Above: To connect Flagstaff and the Union Pacific Railway with the mineral district of Morenci, a trans–Mogollon Rim rail line was proposed in 1883. Thirty-five miles of track heading southeast out of Flagstaff were laid and a tunnel was started through the Rim. However, before the three-thousand-foot tunnel was completed, the project went bankrupt. Right: Woods Canyon is one of many deep, rugged canyons that hampered early travel through the Red Rock–Sacred Mountain area.

Palmer and his soldiers, were back in northern Arizona in 1867–68 traveling along the thirty-fifth parallel to trace out a route for extending the Union Pacific Railway from Fort Wallace in Kansas to the Pacific. With the party was the noted Civil War photographer Alexander Gardner, who took some of the earliest photographs of the San Francisco Peaks.

The close of the nineteenth century witnessed the end of the major government surveys and the beginning of significant scientific inquiry into the local natural and human history.

Jesse Walter Fewkes, a man of many talents, a former student of Louis Agassiz's, and a biology assistant to Alexander Agassiz (Louis's son), became, in his words, " . . . profoundly interested in ethnological problems, especially of the Pueblos" after a trip out West. Several years later, Fewkes was invited to conduct archaeological exploration in Arizona for the Smithsonian Institution.

During the summer of 1895, Fewkes, accompanied by a cook and a photographer, traveled from Prescott to Camp Verde where he visited "cavate dwellings" of "troglodytic" inhabitants before heading up the Verde River to Beaver Creek. There he examined the ruins at Montezuma's Castle and Montezuma's Well, both named by early pioneers who mistakenly thought the Aztecs had lived here.

From Beaver Creek, the party crossed the divide near Beaverhead to Oak Creek and camped at the Schurman Ranch. Here Fewkes studied the "house ruins, fortifications, and aboriginal irrigation canals." Then the group went into the Red Rock Country and did some excavating at the cliff houses Fewkes named Palatki and Honanki. Such structures, he thought, indicated the inhabitants were " . . . subject to attack by powerful nomadic tribes." Subsequent research has proven this false, and the mystery of constructing cliff houses remains. Fewkes also believed all of the pictographs on the cliffs were of fairly recent Apache origin; he would no doubt be surprised to learn that some date back several thousand years. He predicted in his field report that the beauty of the red rocks and Oak Creek would someday lure tourists here. If only he could see it now!

Three decades later, at age seventy-six, Fewkes began to excavate Elden Pueblo, a large ruin at the base of Mount Elden on the northeast outskirts of Flagstaff. Locals often herded stock or sheep directly over the ruin unaware that it was a major archaeological site.

The excavation generated considerable public attention, which led Fewkes to hope the site would be designated a national monument. Unfortunately, over the years, the site fell back into disrepair. A few rooms were examined in 1967 by Northern Arizona University archaeologists, but they generally regarded the site to be of little significance. However, since 1978, work done cooperatively between the Coconino National Forest and the Museum of Northern Arizona has yielded many unusual artifacts at Elden Pueblo, including double bowls and a ceramic effigy considered to be a pregnant pronghorn antelope, as well as a great deal of new information about the latter-day Sinagua.

The pueblo was built over an older pithouse village between A.D. 1130 and 1200. One particularly large room, unusual for such pueblos, may have been a community meeting place. Indeed, the Hopi name for Elden Pueblo is *Pasiwvi,* which means "place of coming together." The particularly exciting discovery of a copper bell in 1986 might indicate trade with Mexico. Excavations continue and the public is allowed to participate.

While some scientists investigated the Red Rock–Sacred Mountain region's ancient cultures, others probed the rocks for clues to the earth's history. After geologist Jules Marcou came other earth scientists such as J. S. Newberry in 1857 and G. K. Gilbert in 1872–73, but these men made a brief examination of this area's geology.

The first comprehensive geologic work on the San Francisco Peaks was performed by a young Ph.D. candidate from Yale, Henry Hollister Robinson. His dissertation was based on field work done between 1901 and 1903, a time when Flagstaff had barely 1,500 residents, but, according to Robinson, "All the most important points of interest in the field may be reached without difficulty by wagon."

While the geologists were peering at the rocky ground and trying to make geologic sense out of the chaos, Percival Lowell and his cohorts were exploring the cosmos. Less than ten years before, Lowell, a Boston Brahman, millionaire, mathematician, and astronomer, had sent

---

1857 to 1859: Edward F. Beale and his men survey and build a wagon road across northern Arizona
▲

1867 to 1868: William Jackson Palmer traces route for Union Pacific Railway
▲

1889: C. Hart Merriam camps at Little Springs and begins the investigations that will lead to his Life Zone Theory
▲

1894: Percival Lowell establishes astronomical observatory in Flagstaff
▲

astronomer Andrew Ellicott Douglass to scout for a good location for a telescope.

After investigating many locations, including Tombstone, Tucson, Tempe, and Prescott, Douglas chose Flagstaff as the best place for "seeing," an intrinsic quality of the air that refers not only to its clarity but steadiness as well. Unfortunately, the bitter, heavy winter of 1894–95 so discouraged Lowell that he resumed his search for the perfect telescope site. He traveled to Mexico, the Sahara Desert, and the Andes, but by 1896 he decided that Flagstaff was indeed the best place, not only for "seeing" but also for hotel accommodations.

In a forty-foot dome atop a low mesa just west of town, Lowell installed a twenty-four-inch refractor telescope (in which a two-foot-diameter lens focuses the image down a long tube to where an eyepiece or instrument can be placed). The observatory was soon ready for Lowell to study his prime astronomical interest: Mars. He was convinced that intelligent life existed on the red planet, because of dark lines on the planet's surface that he thought were built canals. He pointed to the summit of the San Francisco Peaks as an example of a place, though harsh in climate and with little oxygen, that supported life. Surely life could evolve under the most austere conditions. He never speculated what form that life might be, a point missed by the public and press, who were dreaming up visions of little green Martians.

A more earthly admiration was Lowell's love affair with the San Francisco Peaks. In his Flagstaff home, the Baronial Mansion atop Mars Hill (also called Observatory Mesa), Lowell designed "windows," or cut-outs, in the interior walls so the mountains could be seen from a variety of rooms.

Lowell was also an amateur botanist and enjoyed exploring Oak Creek and Sycamore canyons for plant specimens. One species of ash that he collected seemed to be an intermediate form between *Fraxinus quadrangulata*, an eastern species, and *Fraxinus anomala*, the typical desert ash of the Southwest. It was given the scientific name *Fraxinus lowellii*.

While studying the huge magnetic storms on the sun's surface known as sunspots, astronomer Douglass became intrigued by the possible relationship between sunspots and weather and between weather and the growth rings of trees. He sampled logs in the local timber yard and discovered that higher sunspot activity seemed to correlate with increased rainfall, which in turn induced greater growth (wider rings) in some of the Southwest's trees. Thus a record of sunspot activity was indirectly recorded in the patterns of tree rings.

To study older ring patterns, Douglass began to take samples of timber from ancient archaeological sites. Not only did this yield further information for his primary studies but it also allowed the dating of the ruins. Douglass, unwittingly, founded the new science of dendrochronology, or tree-ring dating.

Others of Lowell's assistants would distinguish themselves and the observatory. By examining the light emitted from distant white nebulae (now known as distinct galaxies or clusters of stars), Vesto Melvin Slipher discovered that they are moving away from us and each other at a very high rate of speed. His velocities were later used in equations to show that the universe is expanding, a basic tenet of modern astronomy.

Around the turn of the century, Lowell hired five Harvard mathematicians who spent seven years calculating a probable orbit for a hypothetical Planet X. Lowell believed that another planet existed beyond Neptune, which was the outermost known member of our solar system at the time. Lowell died in 1916 not having discovered a new planet.

In January, 1929, Slipher hired an amateur astronomer from Kansas, Clyde Tombaugh, to assist in the search. Tombaugh was to systematically take photographs of the night sky. A year later, Tombaugh took photos of the night sky on January 23 and 29 using the thirteen-inch A. Lawrence Lowell telescope. On February 18, he began to compare them with a blink comparator, an instrument that allows a brief look at one photo then changes to the second then back to the first. If any object had moved between the two nights, it would appear to jump back and forth through the eyepiece. One tiny spot of light jumped and proved to be a new planet, Lowell's Planet X. The newly discovered planet was named Pluto, a fitting name because it followed the custom of naming planets for Roman gods and goddesses, and because the first two

1895: Archaeologist Jess Walter Fewkes studies Sinagua ruins on Red Rock Country ▲

1899: Fewkes predicts future popularity of area ▲

1930: Harold S. Colton founds the Museum of Northern Arizona to promote the study of the natural and cultural history of the area ▲

1992: Up to 7 million tourists visit the Red Rock–Sacred Mountain area yearly ▲

Left: By the 1870s, the first Anglo pioneers of the Red Rock–Sacred Mountain area were settling along Oak Creek and the base of the Mogollon Rim. Above: Surveyors, escorted by General William Jackson Palmer and his soldiers, were in northern Arizona in 1867–68, traveling along the 35th parallel to trace out a route for extending the Union Pacific Railway from Fort Wallace, Kansas, to the Pacific Ocean. Right: Archaeologist Jesse Walter Fewkes predicted in 1895 that the beauty of the red rocks and Oak Creek would someday lure tourists here. The forest service predicts that annual visitation to the Red Rock Country will reach seven million in the next few years.

Many of the early settlers in Oak Creek Canyon planted apple orchards; surplus fruit was taken to markets in Flagstaff and Jerome. Late spring snow storms occasionally threatened the crop.

Above: Pioneer residents John Jim Thompson and Laura McBride added their names to Oak Creek Canyon's walls; unfortunately, they chose to write their names over prehistoric pictographs. Left: Sedona oldtimers insist that Cathedral Rock near Red Rock Crossing on lower Oak Creek was originally named Courthouse Butte but an 1886 survey done by the General Land Office inadvertently switched the name.

letters were the initials of Percival Lowell.

Exploration of the cosmos led back to earth. During the 1960s, astronauts scheduled to go to the moon came to the Flagstaff area to study volcanic rocks. When Neil Armstrong took his giant step on the moon, he could see the surface was made of basically the same kind of basaltic lava prominent on the San Francisco Peaks volcanic field.

Another early scientist who fell under the Peaks' spell was Dr. Harold S. Colton, a zoologist from the University of Pennsylvania and described by biographer Jimmy Miller as having ". . . acceptable genealogical roots, a privileged economic status, and an intellectual elitism. . . ." During their honeymoon in 1912, Colton and his bride, Mary Russell, toured the Southwest and climbed the San Francisco Peaks. Fourteen years later, the Coltons settled in Flagstaff. Colton remarked, "For the biologist, the San Francisco Peaks are classical ground for here C. Hart Merriam worked out his life zone theory. . . ." Two years later, Colton founded the Museum of Northern Arizona to promote the study of the natural and cultural history of this area and the Colorado Plateau. Colton and his research center have become world famous for their studies and collections of the region's geology, archaeology, anthropology, flora, and fauna.

Colton actively participated in research until his death at age eighty-nine in 1970. His beautiful home, constructed of local malpais rock, ponderosa pine, and Douglas fir, still stands in the forest just north of Flagstaff. A huge picture window in the living room magnificently frames the San Francisco Peaks.

Numerous scientists have been drawn to the Red Rock–Sacred Mountain region. The area continues to be a wellspring of scientific inquiry. One of the most recent additions to encourage these endeavors is the construction of a forest research center. The Southwest Forestry Sciences Complex on the Northern Arizona University Campus will house the School of Forestry and the Arizona research operations of the Forest Service. One of the complex's main objectives will be to blend science and education to resolve critical natural resource issues in the Southwest.

Over four centuries ago, the Spanish conquistadors came to Red Rock–Sacred Mountain Country searching for mineral wealth but returned home empty-handed. Two and a half centuries later, trappers were disappointed in the area's scarcity of beaver. A few decades later, U.S. government surveyors were mostly concerned with where to build trails, wagon roads, and railroads through the region to move people across northern Arizona to "better" places like California. Only in the last century have we begun to appreciate the remarkable cultural and natural resources of the Red Rock–Sacred Mountain region. Scientists have opened our eyes to the true riches and rewards of this area.

The Red Rock–Sacred Mountain area is a land of contrasts and diversity. From Sedona, at the mouth of Oak Creek Canyon, to the summit of the San Francisco Peaks, north of Flagstaff, one gains nearly eight thousand feet in elevation and passes from desert grassland through woodland and forest to alpine tundra, all in a horizontal distance of about thirty-five miles.

LIFE ZONES

TAKE A DRIVE FROM Sedona up through Oak Creek
Canyon to Flagstaff, then continue on to the San Francisco Peaks and up the Snow Bowl Road. At the Snow Bowl
Lodge, take the ski lift to the timberline on Agassiz Peak.
You can't help but notice the striking changes in vegetation that occur along this route. If you stop often, which
I highly recommend, and look and listen, you might
discern some of the native inhabitants—a tiny side-
blotched lizard doing territorial push-ups on a boulder
in the desert grassland around Sedona, the harsh *check-
check-check-check* call of a scrub jay in the pinyon-juniper
woodland, the downward tail-flicking activity of a black
phoebe along Oak Creek, a blur of blue and black from
a crested Steller's jay winging through the ponderosa pine
forest, a mule deer bounding off through a shimmering

aspen grove, or a flash of the white tail feathers on a water
pipit skipping among the timberline boulders.

Changes in plant and animal communities over
latitudinal and altitudinal distances drew the attention of
Clinton Hart Merriam a little over a hundred years ago.

Merriam, a biologist with the U.S. Biological Survey,
came west in 1889 ostensibly to study the "scientific
. . . and economic importance . . . of a region com-
prehending a diversity of physical and climatic conditions," and discovered "unexpected generalizations concerning the relationships of the life areas of North
America."

Merriam long had had an interest in the distribution
of plant and animal communities. His father's extensive
scientific library whetted Merriam's curiosity. Hart, as his

family called him, was especially intrigued by naturalist Alexander von Humboldt's discourse on the different zones of vegetation observed in an ascent of the Andes of South America.

While Merriam was growing up in New York state, the teenager's devotion to hunting sometimes led to the exclusion of other responsibilities. When Hart was thirteen, he was reproached by the family minister for shooting squirrels rather than attending Sunday services. A spirited Hart decided to remove a critical board on a bridge, sending the parson and his carriage into a stream and the horse running home.

At the age of sixteen, Merriam was selected to accompany the 1872 Hayden Survey of Yellowstone and the Rocky Mountains as their naturalist. This stroke of good fortune came about as a result of Merriam's father having introduced the young scientist to Spencer F. Baird, then assistant secretary of the Smithsonian Institution. Baird was quite taken with the young boy's knowledge of natural history and skill in preparing museum specimens.

The expedition to the West fired Merriam's enthusiasm for biology. And although he returned to school for more formal training (at Baird's persuasion) and eventually obtained a medical degree (naturalists were often physicians in the nineteenth century), Merriam's passion was for natural history field work. After six years of practicing medicine, he came to the conclusion that he was ". . . throwing [his] life away for nothing."

In 1885 Merriam accepted the post of ornithologist with the U.S. Department of Agriculture's Division of Entomology. Merriam had been hired to study the role of insectivorous birds in combating crop insect pests. He lobbied to turn his position and office into a biological survey of the entire United States. Though never completed, the objectives of the survey were "to discover and describe hitherto unknown species of North American animals," mostly mammals, and to conduct biogeographical studies. The latter goal plus a six-hundred-dollar grant from the U.S. Secretary of Agriculture (perhaps one of the last inexpensive and cost-effective programs funded by the federal government) brought Merriam to the San Francisco Peaks.

The train pulled into the Flagstaff station on July 26, 1889. Dr. Merriam and his wife, Elizabeth, could finally stretch their legs after the six-day train ride from Washington, D.C. The following day Merriam's chief field assistant, Vernon Bailey, arrived from Albuquerque. The three spent the next several days, as noted by Bailey, "fitting out," buying horses, hiring "Judge" Carruthers as cook and handyman, and "bird shooting around the town."

The Merriams, Bailey, and Carruthers set out for Little Springs, located on the northwest flank of the San Francisco Peaks. Camp was pitched, as Bailey described, ". . . in a grove of aspens and pines, on a knoll just northwest of the spring. . . . I am . . . in one of the grandest mountain counties in the world." For the next two months, this lovely spot would be their base camp. Bailey reported that "The Dr. [Merriam] don't looks so old as he did last summer, I suppose because his wife makes him shave, don't look much older than I do. His wife is a very pleasant little woman with yellow hair & big blue eyes. . . . We have 4 tents up, one for a kitchen & the cook, one for the Dr. & his wife, one for skinning our specimens, & my little tent all for myself. It is quite a camp for only 4 small people."

Occasionally locals would come for a visit. Bailey noted, "A party of 8 or 10 came up from Flagstaff last night to stay over Sunday. They were the upper crust of town and some of them seem to be nice people." Two additional scientists also came to Merriam's camp. In mid-August, Professor F. H. Knowlton, a government botanist from Washington, came and stayed the rest of the season collecting plants. In early September, Dr. Leonhard Stejneger, curator of reptiles at the U.S. National Museum, joined the group. He had come to Arizona not only to collect reptiles but also in hope that the warm, dry climate would cure him of a lung ailment. (The Sacred Mountain's climate must have helped: Stejneger lived to be ninety-two, another fifty-four years!)

Scientific excursions were made to the Grand Canyon, the Hopi Mesas across the Painted Desert (a harrowing and almost fatal excursion when the group ran out of drinking water), Walnut Canyon, O'Leary Peak, and, of course, the San Francisco Peaks. On August 23, Merriam, Bailey, and Knowlton set off to climb to the summit.

Bailey wrote of this journey: "We rode up to 11,000 feet to timber line & left our horse and Mr. Knowlton, and M[erriam] & I went on afoot. M. got about 1,000 feet higher & I carried the barometer to the top at 13,000 feet. It is the highest that I have ever been and I could not get any too much breath. The scenery was grand beyond my power of description. To stand on a peak of a volcano 13,000 feet high & look across desert & to other mountains hundreds of miles away & down into the tops of five hundred smaller craters, some of them over 10,000 feet high, is scenery on a large scale. I could look into the ca$on of the Colorado, could see lots of lakes & hundreds of miles of pine forest. There was snow on the north slope & only moss and a few little stunted plants reached the summit. The [Engelmann] spruce & a species of mountain pine [the

Although C. Hart Merriam's life zones fairly well define the "big picture" of plant communities such as desert, woodlands, and forest, there are many micro-habitats as well. One example is the bigtooth maple (Acer grandidentatum) community found in some of the steep, shady drainages along the Mogollon Rim. These small trees are usually inconspicuous until the autumn, when their crimson leaves create splashes of color on the canyon walls.

bristlecone] become scrubby & almost creeping & finally disappear 2,000 feet below the top. The top is all loose stones as steep as they will lay. . . .''

Merriam recorded the climb in his journal: "At timber line we heard a great noise in the fallen timber & on looking saw 8 or 9 mountain sheep which followed one another in a single line up to the ridge over which they disappeared. . . . The spruce or balsam forest is very dense & there is much fallen timber. Except for the north crest of the spur the rocks are very bad. The new pine & new spruce continue to timber line, where they exist as gnarled & flattened depauperate bent to the south. . . . We saw two golden eagles there at about 12,000 feet. . . . Knowlton collected more than 40 species of plants."

Several days later, Merriam and Bailey climbed the mountain again and Bailey remained there to hunt. Merriam wrote on August 28: "Elizabeth, Knowlton, & I went up the mt. We went (rode on horseback most of the way) from Little Spring to Bailey's camp just below timber line in two hours. Joined Bailey & climbed to the top of the main peak. Had a brief hail storm while there. Saw . . . a great stretch of country in every direction. . . . A pair of peregrine falcons seem to have their headquarters in some high cliffs in the crater. . . . Knowlton got a lot of new plants & returned to Little Spring. Elizabeth & I stayed up on the mt. with Vernon Bailey. We ate broiled eagle for supper."

This last confession only hints at Merriam's catholic tastes. Bailey remarked, "Skunks & cats are his [Merriam] favorite meat & he is specially fond of eagle." While Bailey didn't share his colleague's palate, he did respect the man: "He [Merriam] is a queer old chap, but a splendid fellow to camp with, always does his share & never shirks the dirty or hard work."

The Merriams left for Washington, D.C., on October 1. Knowlton journeyed to San Francisco and Stejneger traveled to Prescott where he was joined by Bailey ten days later.

During those ten days, Bailey remained on the Peaks, finishing his mapping of the altitudinal ranges of various tree species. His final letter from Little Springs to home said in part, "A large part of our work here has been getting the upper and lower limit of the different species of trees & coloring them on the Geol. Survey map sheet. You know how those contour lines show the altitudes on the maps, and we color the tree zones by these lines after we find out the limit of the ranges of the species. The maps are to be made showing the mammal and bird zones & that will show how they correspond with plant zones. It is easier to map the trees than animals; so we do that first

Paintbrush and lupine flourish in the High Country.

& the others will be mapped later from our notes. It is all splendid work & is entirely new–originated by Dr. Merriam."

The biologists had also discovered twenty mammals new to science. "I asked the Dr. last night when he was going to publish his book on mammals & he said when I get done getting new species for it."

As the field season ended, Bailey mused, "The popples [aspen] are like fall gold & are scattered among the pines so that the yellow and black-green of the pines makes a rich contrast. The old mountain looks quite gay. There is frost often . . . it is warm enough here when the sun shines, but in the evening we get pretty close to the fire & keep a big fire too."

From his studies on the Peaks and explorations into the depths of the Grand Canyon and the parched Painted Desert, Merriam devised his renowned "life zones." His original seven life zones – Desert, Pinyon, Neutral or Pine, Canadian, Hudsonian, Sub-alpine, and Alpine – were delimited by temperature. Merriam's "laws of temperature control" theoretically governed distribution of plants and animals. He believed that animals and plants were restricted in their northern (or highest altitudinal) distribution by the total quantity of heat available during the growth and reproduction season. Their southern (or lowest altitudinal) range was delineated by their tolerance to the mean temperature of the six hottest weeks of the year. He stated unequivocally that "temperature and humidity are the most important causes governing distribution, and temperature is more potent than humidity." (On average, temperature decreases three to five degrees Fahrenheit per one thousand feet gain in elevation; precipitation increases approximately four to five inches.)

Merriam's dogmatic conclusions would eventually be his undoing as a biologist. Other biologists began to point out that a combination of environmental factors – climatic, physical, and biological – determined plant distribution. Furthermore, each species responded to these environmental factors in its own unique fashion. Discrete zones maintain their validity only if a few of the dominant plants are considered.

Modern ecologists, such as Robert Whittaker, point out that each species is distributed in response to environmental factors independently of others. No two groups of species have exactly the same limits; thus, when examined in detail, no recognizable natural communities seem to exist. Yet when we step back and look at the "big picture," Merriam's life zones seem to be real entities. It is a bit like a rainbow. Close up the spectrum is a continual

*Above: This species of barrel cactus (*Echinocactus polycephalus*) growing on Strawberry Crater, a cinder cone north-east of Flagstaff, is usually found at much lower elevations in the Grand Canyon area. How this individual arrived at this loftier, more southern locale and how it manages to survive here are the types of questions pondered by modern ecologists. Left: According to Merriam's life zone concept, cactus, such as this prickly pear (*Opuntia phaeacantha*), would be typical of the desert zone. However, today's ecologists realize that many environmental factors—climatic, physical, and biological—determine plant distribution. For instance, this species of prickly pear cactus has been found growing at elevations ranging from 1,000 to over 7,500 feet.*

gradient of color from red to green to violet, but from a distance, we perceive definite bands of color.

Despite these challenges to the life zone concept, Merriam would not budge. And while Merriam's broad, continental generalizations were incorrect, his meticulous work on the San Francisco Peaks remains a classic ecological study and forms a cornerstone of modern biogeography. For his extensive studies of mammals, he has been called "the father of modern American mammalogy." And in 1883 he helped organize the American

Ornithologists' Union, whose main purpose is to designate official common and scientific names for birds.

Merriam left the Biological Survey in 1910 and spent the last thirty-two years of his life studying obscure and vanishing California Indian cultures. He died at age eighty-six. Although Merriam ventured off onto other scientific tangents, his life zone concept is still a useful interpretation of the diverse plant and animal communities found in the Red Rock–Sacred Mountain area.

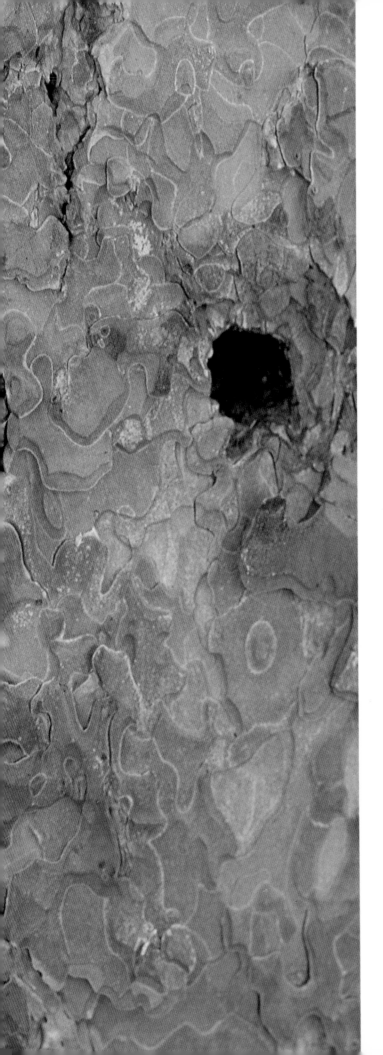

The short-horned lizard (Phrynosoma douglassi), sometimes mistakenly called the horny toad, is the most cold-tolerant of the seven western species of horned lizards, and has been observed at nearly eleven thousand feet on the San Francisco Peaks.

Above: Hedgehog cactus (Echinocereus triglochidiatus) appears in the ponderosa pine forest on rocky, south-facing slopes. Left: During July and August of 1889, C. Hart Merriam and his party camped near Little Springs on the northwest flank of the San Francisco Peaks. Right: The golden-mantled ground squirrel (Spermophilus lateralis) resides in the conifer forest.

SQUIRRELS, PINES, AND TRUFFLES

T HE ANNOYING WHINE OF a chain saw rips through the air. A contractor is felling another mature ponderosa in the small lot across the road from my house a few miles south of the San Francisco Peaks. Seven of the old magnificent trees are to be removed so another house can be built. I feel ambivalent about the building project because, while I understand the desire of the property owner to build and live in a house, I mourn the loss of hundreds of years of organic growth represented by those trees. I, too, live in a house of wood, a house built in the forest, so it would be hypocritical of me to condemn my neighbor. But I am concerned for the wildlife, especially the Abert squirrels, that had counted on that bit of forest for food and shelter.

In 1851, Captain Lorenzo Sitgreaves, with the help of mountain man Antoine Leroux, was attempting to locate a route across northern Arizona to connect the settlements in New Mexico with those of California. As was customary in that era, the expedition's physician, Samuel Woodhouse, was also the chief naturalist. Woodhouse was the first to note "a singular species of striped squirrel" in the ponderosa pine forest around the San Francisco Peaks. Woodhouse named this squirrel after an amateur naturalist and avid bird collector, Colonel J. W. Abert, then head of the U.S. Corps of Engineers. Colonel Abert had explored the squirrel's eastern range on the east slope of the Rocky Mountains in 1845–46 and perhaps had seen the animal there. Less than a century later, humans had invaded most of the squirrel's home range.

While camped near the base of the San Francisco Peaks on Christmas Day, 1853, zoologist C. B. R. Kennerly (who was with another government survey party, this one led by Amiel Weeks Whipple) remarked, ". . . we found in great numbers the beautiful tufted squirrel, (*Sciurus aberti*), and admired its gracefulness as it leaped from tree to tree, or passed swiftly over the frozen snow. . . ." During the winter, Aberts have long tassels of hair extending beyond the tips of their ears, giving them an almost comical and decidedly cute appearance. There is some evidence that the tassels are involved in sexual display; the tassels tend to be longer in males and are lost by pregnant females.

Although the high country winters can be quite severe, the squirrel never goes into a deep hibernation. Instead, the squirrel enters a state of torpor or slowed-down metabolism for short periods and may emerge from its nest on sunny winter days. Arousal is probably triggered by increasing metabolic wastes in the squirrel's system.

I hear the splintering of wood, breaking of branches, and a tremendous thud as another old tree crashes to the ground. Somewhere high in the crown of one of those doomed trees was an Abert squirrel nest. The nest, constructed mostly of pine branch ends six inches to two feet in length, is placed in the protected interior of a group of ponderosa pines whose crowns have interlocked. These trees tend to be fifteen to twenty inches in diameter and exceed one hundred years in age. Occasionally nests are built in the abnormal growths of pine twigs known as "witches' brooms." The "prefabricated broom nests" are usually the result of an infection of dwarf mistletoe (*Arceuthobium vaginatum*). The nest is built thirty to fifty feet above the ground, about three-fourths of the way up the tree. The squirrels take advantage of solar heating by placing the nest on the south to southwest side of the tree.

The relationship between Southwestern ponderosa pine forests and the Abert squirrel goes far beyond one of sheer convenience; it's a matter of survival. Northern Arizona University biologists Jack States, Bill Gaud, W. S. Allred, W. S. Austin, and their colleagues have recently begun to unravel the specifics of this interdependence.

During the late spring or early summer, the Abert's favorite food is the green and succulent bean-sized clusters of staminate (male) cones of the ponderosa. These pollen-producing flowers are abundant for only a couple of weeks, so the squirrels are busy clipping the ends of the flower-bearing branches along with the crown of developing needles, eating the flowers, and dropping the remains. Some zoologists believe that the appearance of this high-energy food source may be a key factor in triggering breeding in the squirrel.

During the time the surviving male cones are getting ready to produce pollen, the ovulate (female) flowers develop into stobili (conelets). The conelets are not eaten by the squirrels but when fertilized the following spring begin to grow into cones. The squirrels cut the maturing cones, remove the scales, and relish the small pine seeds and the surrounding moist tissue. The squirrels discard the cone centers like miniature corn cobs. Not every pine provides a good meal, though. In the Flagstaff area, only ponderosas greater than sixty years old are good cone-producers.

Some twenty-three species of hypogeous (subterranean) fungi and mushrooms associated with pine trees become an important food source during the summer and early fall. "Truffles" of the genera *Gautieria, Rhizopogon,* and *Morchella* are the most consistently available high-quality food resource and at times comprise 75 to 100 percent of the squirrels' diet. The fungi are also a significant source of moisture for the squirrels in the typically dry forest.

Unlike most tree squirrels, Aberts do not store food in large caches for the winter, but they occasionally will bury an individual cone or bits of fungi in a shallow pit. A side-benefit of digging holes seems to be in providing conduits for water penetration into the root system of the tree. With the onset of winter, the squirrels rely on the inner bark and apical (branch end) buds from the ponderosa as food. When feeding on inner bark, the Abert bites off selected branches and then clips off the very end of the branch with its cluster of needles, allowing it to fall to the ground. The squirrel takes the remaining segment, strips off the outer bark, and eats the inner bark (phloem and xylem). The unconsumed woody parts are dropped to the forest floor where decomposition will eventually return nutrients such as carbon and nitrogen to the soil. The clippings of terminal needle clusters, which look like pine needle bouquets, and peeled twigs on the forest floor are obvious evidence that Abert squirrels inhabit the area.

Other foods eaten by the squirrels include the dwarf mistletoe, insects, various greens, pine needles, and seeds from my bird feeder. Gambel oak acorns provide an important mast crop.

All this eating of pine products has worried some foresters. In 1908, a young forester by the name of Gustaf Adalph Pearson was sent by the Forest Service to Arizona to study the life cycle of the ponderosa pine. Pearson had grown up on the treeless Great Plains where trees were viewed as a symbol of wealth. He came to Arizona with almost a missionary zeal to convert the land to productive forest. Within a year, Pearson had established the Fort

The timber industry claims that there are more ponderosa pines now than ever before. This is true, but most of the trees occur in dog-hair thickets of small-diametered pines that have developed primarily as a result of fire suppression. Before the forest service began to fight fires, the forest averaged seventeen to twenty pines per acre. The present forest around Flagstaff averages 851 trees per acre.

Valley Experimental Station at the base of the San Francisco Peaks.

Pearson observed that the pine reproduction around Flagstaff was poor both in virgin stands and in areas already logged. Southwest of Flagstaff on the Prescott National Forest, he saw dense stands of young trees that he thought would grow into vigorous mature timber. At the time, he did not realize the important roles that weather conditions, fire, and other environmental factors play in ponderosa reproduction and growth. Furthermore, it was unknown at the time that climatic conditions in this area only rarely conspire to allow significant pine regeneration. The last such time for the Coconino National Forest was 1919 (eleven years after Pearson arrived in the Southwest). He wrongly concluded that reducing Abert squirrel populations and controlling fires would help the Flagstaff forest yield more timber. Pearson, however, did amass an incredible amount of biological information about ponderosa pines, and he established study plots where some forty thousand trees were measured. One such plot, today's Pearson Natural Area, contains one of the few remaining virgin stands on the Coconino National Forest. Here over six thousand pines have been measured and monitored at five- or ten-year intervals starting in 1920. This amazing collection of baseline information should prove invaluable to future foresters.

Even earlier, in an 1899 report to the Secretary of the Interior, surveyor and geographer Henry Gannett remarked that, "It [the forest] has been remarkably free from fires, a fact doubtless due in great part to its open character and freedom from underbrush." The recurrence, not absence, of fires in producing such open stands would not be appreciated for many years.

Furthermore, the role of the squirrel would not be perceived until the 1980s (and in some respects, is not yet). As mentioned earlier, fungi are associated with the roots of the pine. After the summer rains begin in July, Aberts are attracted by odor to these "truffles," or underground fungi. Threadlike hyphae (analogous to roots in seed plants) of the fungus encase root hairs of the conifer. The fungus is better adapted to absorbing nutrients, particularly nitrogen and phosphate, from the soil than are the tree's roots. The tree's root hairs then absorb the nutrients directly from the fungus. In return, the fungus derives part of its nourishment from the carbon products created by the tree's photosynthesis. Poor soils, so typical of the ponderosa pine forest, are the preferred habitat of the fungus. This mutually beneficial relationship is further strengthened by hormones secreted by the fungus that stimulate root growth, thus increasing the surface area for more fungal growth.

By eating truffles and defecating spores, the Abert squirrel is the main dispersal mechanism for hypogeous fungal spores.

So important is this combination of hyphae and pine roots (which botanists call mycorrhizae) to the perpetuation of the ponderosa forest that foresters are beginning to artificially inoculate pine roots with hyphae to stimulate pine growth in poor soils. Nearly every species of vascular plants (those that possess specialized cells for transporting food, water, and minerals; in other words, what most laypeople would call a plant) has at least one species of fungi symbiotically associated with its roots as mycorrhizae. The ties and bonds of different species are indeed miraculous and vastly important to the perpetuation of life.

Ponderosa forest ranges from northern Mexico to British Columbia along the Rocky and Pacific Coast mountains. Utah State University Associate Professor of Forestry Ronald Lanner states that the ponderosa pine's range "defines the American West." In the Southwest, ponderosa are the most common tree between 5,500 feet and 8,500 feet in elevation. Despite the seemingly less than ideal growing conditions for ponderosa, Flagstaff is in the midst of the largest contiguous ponderosa pine forest in the world, a forest some three hundred miles long and thirty miles wide.

The adventurous Scottish botanist David Douglas (for whom the fir is named) was the first non-Indian to recognize ponderosa as a "new species" and to name it. (Interestingly, a quarter century earlier, government explorer Meriwether Lewis had noticed this species of pine but failed to collect it or name it.) Douglas was so impressed by the ponderous two-hundred-foot giants, growing in the Pacific Northwest where he was exploring in the 1820s, that he christened them with their common name. In the Southwest, ponderosa generally grow eighty to 125 feet tall, only a fraction of the size of their Northwest relatives. This shorter stature is a function of the Southwest's drier climate. Here ponderosa have a straight trunk two to three feet in diameter, but occasionally achieve a three-and-a-half-foot or larger diameter and a height of 150 feet or more.

The bark on young trees less than a foot in diameter tends to be blackish and furrowed into ridges, whereas larger, mature trunks (sexual maturity is a function of an individual tree's physiology and growth rate, so maturity may be reached anywhere from forty years to over two hundred years!) become cinnamon brown and irregularly

Acorn woodpeckers cache acorns (these are from a Gambel oak) in holes they drill in large, mature ponderosa pines.

62

fissured into a jig-saw puzzle of large, flat, scaly plates that will flake off like mica. The inner, non-living heartwood is hard and reddish brown; the outer, living, soft sapwood is white to pale yellow. When the sap is flowing, the mature tree trunks have a delightful vanilla or butterscotch scent.

The oldest ponderosa pine ever recorded was 1,047 years old when it was felled in the early 1900s in Colorado. More typically the pines grow to be 350 to 500 years old before succumbing to disease or some other natural disaster. The largest Arizona ponderosa was cut on the Coconino National Forest in 1920. This behemoth was 640 years old and still six feet across some forty feet up from its base. Currently the tallest known living ponderosa in Arizona is a 120-foot tree in Yavapai County. Sadly, the biggest Arizona ponderosas were the first to be cut down.

The ponderosa in northern and central Arizona are considered the *scopulorum* variety, which has the typical three needles to a bundle (that is, three needles attach to the branch at a common point) and differs little from the ponderosa of the Pacific Coast states. However, in the higher mountains of southern and southeastern Arizona, the ponderosa (variety *arizonica*) have five needles to a fascicle (bundle) and shorter cones.

Lumberers consider the ponderosa the most important sawtimber in Arizona and New Mexico and second only to Douglas fir in the United States. Lumber for buildings, crates, millwork, caskets, furniture, toys, veneer, railroad ties, fuel, and paper comes from ponderosa. The pine has also been used in the manufacture of turpentine, chewing gum, crayons, printing ink, disinfectants, shoe polish, soap, shatter-proof glass, hairbrush bristles, explosives, photo film, and hundreds of other products. Today, ponderosa from the Coconino National Forest primarily provides lumber, paper, fiberboard, and fence posts.

Pioneers and Native Americans found additional uses for ponderosa such as making cough syrup by pounding green pine needles into a pulp and mixing the juice with honey. Pine juice was also used to rinse the hair; pine gum was spread over cuts. The inner bark was occasionally eaten. Following a special ceremony, members of the Sword Swallowers Order of the Great Fire Fraternity of the Zunis would ingest young shoots of ponderosa pine if they wanted their wives to bear sons, but would eat pinyon shoots for a daughter.

Arguably the ponderosa's greatest value is not in its commercial uses but rather as a forest resident, the most important link in the ecological web of the ponderosa pine forest. Over one thousand species of plants and vertebrate animals are in some way related to ponderosa. This figure

The Abert squirrel (Sciurus aberti) *is a key link in the maintenance of a healthy ponderosa pine forest.*

does not include insects and other invertebrates. The ponderosa forest is to a degree unusual in that only one tree species dominates the plant community. Contrast that to a lush Northwestern forest composed of dozens of species of trees or to an Eastern deciduous forest that contains a hundred tree species or more. According to forest scientist Mike Wagner, the ponderosa forest's paucity of tree diversity is partly related to the limited amount of precipitation in the arid Southwest and shorter growing season of the high country where it grows. Where the forest is open, the understory may consist of bunch grasses, wildflowers, and a few scattered shrubs, but as forest density increases, limited sunlight and very acidic soils (caused by the decomposition of pine needles) prevent much understory growth. The nutrient and water requirements of one ponderosa may preclude any other plants from growing within thirty to forty feet around the tree.

Since biological diversity generally translates into more stable ecosystems—that is, ones that are able to withstand slight ecological disturbances better than less diverse ecosystems—ponderosa pine forests, from a biological standpoint, may be considered more vulnerable than the biologically "complex" Eastern or Northwestern forests.

Another element to consider when speculating why this region's forest is essentially monospecific is the continued "disruption" of the ecosystem by periodic wildfire. Lanner asserts, "ponderosa pine is born of fire." Periodic lightning-caused fires (historically on the Coconino National Forest fires occurred every two to ten years) clear away the deep, dry litter of needles and decaying humus so seedling roots can find moist mineral soil. Fire also kills other plants that might shade the pine seedling and thus inhibit growth. Once a pine stand is established, fire continues to influence its development. Light fuels are consumed, thus preventing a hot, crowning conflagration. As a relatively cool-burning ground fire eddies up and around the lee side of a tree, a Gothic arch-shaped burn is formed in the cambium. The deadwood within these so called "cat-face scars" (not to be confused with the colloquialism for bulldozer-inflicted scars, "CAT-faces") may become the home of large, shiny black carpenter ants. The ants excavate intricate anastomosing galleries where they will lay their eggs.

As evidenced in historical descriptions of the high country prior to Smokey Bear's admonitions and active fire suppression by the forest service, natural fires helped establish an open, savannalike forest. Nutrients were released, the thick pine needle litter was removed, and

a good pine seed bed resulted. Fire suppression (about seventy-five years' worth on the Coconino National Forest) has allowed fuels to build up in certain parts of the forest to an alarming level. Even three-inch-thick, corky, fire-resistant bark may not be enough to protect mature pines from a really hot fire. Not only does an intense fire kill most of the trees, but the newly exposed ground is then subject to sheet erosion. Today some natural fires are allowed to burn, and controlled burns are one management tool used by the Forest Service to lessen the danger of large, destructive fires. However, forest scientist Wallace Covington warns that the situation is still critical. He estimates that during pre-settlement times the fuel load was 2.6 tons per acre of forest. Today, the average is twenty-one tons per acre. Combine that figure with the fact that northern Arizona has one of the highest rates in the United States for lightning strikes and you can understand his concern.

Scattered throughout the ponderosa forest are large natural meadows, called parks by the locals. Pines rarely invade these areas because the parks are either too wet as a result of poor drainage due to clay deposits (some of the local volcanic rocks decompose into clay) or too dry because of excessive drainage (such as where volcanic cinders overlay porous limestone).

Once the summer rains come, these parks are ablaze with wildflowers amidst swaying fields of blue grama grass, Arizona fescue, mountain muhly, pine dropseed, needlegrass, mountain brome, Arizona wheatgrass, squirreltail, and the introduced Kentucky bluegrass.

In the past, intensive livestock grazing has led to poor pine regeneration and the creation of more meadows. When the number of animals was greatly reduced as grazing became regulated after the turn of the century, pines quickly invaded the open areas. Dense stands of small trees, called dog-hair thickets, have grown up in these old meadows and have persisted because of fire suppression.

If dog-hair thickets escape burning, their own overcrowded condition creates less vigorous trees. The trees shade each other too much, and there is not enough ground water to go around. As much as one thousand pounds (125 gallons) of water transpires through a pine's needles to produce every pound of wood. Covington states that in pre-settlement time there were only seventeen to twenty trees per acre. Today the forest averages 851 trees per acre, and in some thickets there may be six thousand to ten thousand stunted ponderosas per acre. The enormous amount of water needed for good growth is just not available in this semi-arid country.

These less vigorous trees are more susceptible to

Above: During late spring and early summer, the Abert squirrel's favorite food is the succulent, bean-sized clusters of staminate (male) cones of the ponderosa pine. Right: The role of mushrooms and truffles in the survival of forests has just recently begun to be investigated by scientists. Nearly every species of vascular plant has at least one species of fungi symbiotically associated with its roots.

66

disease and attack by bark beetles. The weakened trees cannot resist invasion by the wood-boring beetles by forcing them out with pitch, and a beetle epidemic may occur. The beetles' natural controls, woodpeckers and nematode parasites, which usually keep beetle outbreaks in check, may be ineffectual. As Wagner has pointed out, "Hundreds of thousands of acres of pine trees died in the past year [1991] in the West because of pine-bark beetles. If we create forests of high density old trees, we almost assume that there will be a large population of pine-bark beetles."

The bark beetles lay eggs between the bark and nutrient-rich wood in the late summer. The eggs hatch into white larvae that feed on the trees through the winter, developing into beetles that fly to attack new trees the next summer. The rice-sized, black bodies of the beetle carry a fungus that grows inside the tree, staining the wood blue and plugging the cells that transport the tree's nutrients. The pine needles then die and turn yellow-brown.

While fostering the destructive work of bark beetles, the extremely dense pine thickets also discourage wildlife. Large animals like deer and elk cannot squeeze through closely packed trees and birds cannot fly between the tangle of branches. The Forest Service would like to see these thickets thinned, but no one currently has a comprehensive plan. In addition, the timber industry complains that it is too expensive to retool for these smaller trees in what they judge an uncertain market.

In the more open parts of the forest where ponderosa are able to grow to sexual maturity, the egg-shaped female flowers are not fertilized the first year that they form. During the following spring, the female conelets open their scales briefly while yellow pollen from male cones drifts on the spring winds. After fertilization, the scales close and the cones grow another four to five inches during the summer. Inside, two winged seeds develop under each scale.

Every few years, particularly when April and May temperatures are above average, ponderosa pines produce enormous seed crops. The tiny winged seeds twirl downward and outward to the ground like miniature helicopters. If not eaten by mountain chickadees, Steller's jays,

nuthatches, sparrows, woodpeckers, porcupines, squirrels, mule deer, or mice, the next spring the seeds on bare, sunny, hot soils germinate and send down long taproots searching for moisture. At least half of a ponderosa's volume is underground. Roots forty to fifty feet in length have been uncovered. Root competition between trees is intense, especially since most of the roots are no farther than eight inches below the surface.

As ponderosa matures, its growth rate slows. In contrast to the pyramidal crown of youth (a pyramid is the most efficient shape for exposing the maximum number of needles to sunlight), the older pine develops a broad, flat or rounded crown, often studded with dead limbs. The needles are shorter on older trees and fewer needles are grown each succeeding year. Fewer cones are produced and the inner bark becomes less nutritious for squirrels. The furrowed, platy bark becomes more smooth.

Eventually the old tree may be struck by lightning, infested with bark beetles or mistletoe, or perhaps killed by fire. Then it may stand another century as a dead barkless snag. In the past, the Forest Service often felled snags in the mistaken belief that they attracted lightning which would lead to a forest fire. But while dead on the outside, snags provide life to the larvae of wood-boring beetles, ants, and wood-decaying fungi which in turn is parasitized by the coral root orchid. Perhaps the hollow trunk will be home for a litter of gray fox pups or a nest of three-toed woodpeckers.

The cutting across the road has stopped. The only sound now is the rushing of the wind through the tops of the remaining pines–the song of the forest. A Steller's jay hops branch to branch down to a fresh stump, cocks its head, and makes a rasping call like someone raking the teeth of a comb, one of the many strange noises these jays make during the breeding season. From the tangle of downed trees, I spy a fluffy gray and white tail slowly waving above a silvery body. The Abert squirrel, too, seems to be examining the wreckage. Will he miss his old home? Will he find a new one? I think I'll go plant a few more pines in my yard as an investment in future squirrel habitat in the Red Rock–Sacred Mountain area.

A frosty ponderosa pine in Sunset Crater National Monument.

Squirreltail (Sitanion hystrix) is a widespread grass in the ponderosa pine forest but is of forage value only before the seeds' long taillike awns mature into stiff threads or after they have been shed. Inset: Natural meadows called parks contain many species of grass including blue grama (Bouteloua gracilis), which is one of northern Arizona's most valuable forage plants for both native animals and livestock.

VANISHING OLD GROWTH

STEPPING INTO A PRISTINE, mature ponderosa pine forest borders on a religious experience. The tall, orange-barked trees shoot straight to the heavens. Between the well-spaced trees, shafts of golden light dance across a carpet of pine needles and soft green grass. Abert squirrels chatter away; mule deer bound through the glades. My friend Tom and I are off to find just such a scene, never mind that it is the middle of winter and snow lies deep across the land.

Our first stop is at the Coconino National Forest's Mormon Lake district office. John Nelson, District Recreation and Land Staff Officer, has told us that he knows of some old growth on Anderson Mesa. On his office wall is a large map of the Mormon Lake district. Nelson points out a couple of what seem to me very tiny areas that may contain

virgin stands of old growth in drainages emptying into Walnut Canyon.

With map in hand, Tom and I are ready. We drive out past what's left (after several years of drought) of Lower Lake Mary and turn up the road leading to telescopes that the U.S. Geologic Survey, Perkins University, and Lowell Observatory have atop Anderson Mesa. We park at the snow-buried turnoff to Marshall Lake, clip on our skis, and head out into the forest.

Our compass course takes us through fairly flat, open country covered with a few big yellow pines (the common forester's term for mature ponderosa), small patches of doghair thickets, and scattered stands of Gambel oak. But this is not a natural old growth stand; numerous weathered, large-diameter stumps clearly indicate that logging occurred here in the past. After a couple of miles, we drop through a tangle of crowded, small pines into a drainage leading north to Walnut Canyon. Most of the medium to large pines have blue lines or numbers painted on their trunks; they are destined for the lumber mill.

As we near the rim of Walnut Canyon, we see on our map that we must climb up and over the ridge to our left to reach the old growth – the virgin, primordial forest of our dreams. The steep slope is rocky and we are forced to remove our skis and walk up the hill. On top are old trees but they, too, have blue painted lines on their trunks. Maybe if we go a little farther.

As we enter the area marked on our map, the nature of the forest changes dramatically. It's not a flat, open forest of mature pines as we imagined but rather steep slopes covered with a mixture of Douglas fir, white fir, a spruce here and there, Rocky Mountain juniper, and some huge pines. To our horror, these large trees are also marked with the dreaded blue lines. (Later, to our relief, Nelson tells us that this particular stand has been removed from the harvest roster.)

Within a few minutes, we have skied and walked the entire old growth stand. It's getting dark and looks like there's a storm moving in – time to head home.

As we ski back to the car, I think about old growth forest. Biologists define many types of old growth in our area – fairly pure stands of ponderosa, mixed conifer stands, mixed pine and oak. There can also be old-stands of pinyon-juniper woodlands, chaparral, and so on. And what about the young trees of today? Given a chance, will they grow and age into the old growth stands of tomorrow?

In the Coconino National Forest Plan, a land and resource plan that guides the direction of the management of the forest for the next decade or so, very rigid and complex guidelines define old growth. No doubt the timber industry has its own concept of old growth, too; perhaps it's a vision of row after row of pines planted like an Iowa cornfield. Obviously, old growth can be many different kinds of forest.

Depending on how one defines old growth and potential old growth, a range of acreages can describe how much old growth remains on the Coconino National Forest. But one aspect that all these diverse visions of old growth have in common is that there used to be more of it in the past, and it is continuing to vanish.

The history of forest management in the Southwest begins only a little over a century ago. The Department of Agriculture and the General Land Office had authority over Arizona's forests when Anglo settlement began in earnest in the mid-1800s, but there was little enforceable

regulation of forestry practices. Theft of timber from public lands was rampant; Arizona was second only to Montana in suspected timber trespass (cutting without permission). Prosecuting suspected thieves was difficult.

Furthermore, an 1887 federal report on Arizona forests described the "destructive [but legal] inroads" from railroads and settlements. Yet the federal government gave nearly eight million acres of public land, much of it in the forested high country of northern Arizona, to the Atlantic and Pacific Railroad to encourage development.

The 1882 arrival of the Atlantic and Pacific Railroad (later to become the Atchison, Topeka & Santa Fe) not only served as an impetus to Flagstaff's growth (the 1880 census counted only sixty-seven residents, compared to 1,500 in 1900) but also sparked the first major commercial logging operation in the area. Flagstaff resident Edward Ayer realized there was a grand business opportunity in supplying wooden ties and bridge timbers to the railroad. His sawmill went into production in the summer of 1882 just two weeks before the tracks arrived.

Five years later, the Riordan brothers, Denis, Timothy, and Michael, bought out Ayer's operation. In those days, anybody with an ax and a saw could cut trees. In an attempt to slow down the denuding of the forest and to gain a firmer grip on the forest land, the influential Riordans lobbied for the establishment of forest preserves. Nineteen years before Arizona would become a state, Denis Riordan proclaimed, "I believe the government ought to withdraw all timber lands it possesses and . . . appoint a competent forester who would make it his sole duty to see that the covering which nature has afforded our mountain tops should be preserved . . . and the time to act is the present. . . . I believe it is the duty of every person who can give the matter thought and . . . influence any one's action . . . to make some endeavor to perpetuate our forest conditions for the benefit of future generations. . . ."

Riordan's idea began to become reality with the passage of the 1891 Creative Act authorizing the president to establish forest preserves from the public domain. Regrettably, another six years passed before the Forest Organic Administration Act spelled out the purpose and intent of forest preserves. (Incidentally, when President Benjamin Harrison proclaimed the first forest preserve, in 1893, the press called his actions "un-democratic" and "un-American.") Another year went by before the forest stretching from the San Francisco Peaks along the Mogollon Rim east to New Mexico was set aside as the Black Mesa Forest Preserve to protect the timber resources and watershed. Irrigators in southern Arizona approved,

Ponderosa tree rings not only reveal the age of the plant but also record the wet and dry years by the width of each growth ring.

72

but miners and ranchers howled. A local newspaper editorial suggested, ". . . hang these U.S. tree agents to the trees that they come to save." A cattleman, Alfred Potter, was chosen to formulate the federal government's grazing policy in order to help placate the dissenters.

Amazingly, it was not until 1905, under the Teddy Roosevelt administration, that a managing agency was founded to oversee the preserves. The fledgling Forest Service inherited forests that in some cases had been so intensively harvested and abused that to this day they have not recovered.

Most of the few virgin stands of ponderosa pine have survived because of oversight or rugged topography. The only major virgin stand left in Arizona is on the Kaibab Plateau, the Grand Canyon's North Rim, within Grand Canyon National Park. Differences between the virgin forest and the adjacent logged national forest are clearly evident to astronauts six hundred miles up in space.

Along with the harvesting of trees came the grazing of livestock. Before 1900, hundreds of thousands of sheep, thousands of horses, and over 100,000 cattle grazed the high country of northern Arizona. Tall bunchgrasses were replaced by plants less palatable to livestock. Denuding the land accelerated erosion. The Rio de Flag, which runs from the San Francisco Peaks through Flagstaff, started to entrench itself by 1890. Twenty-five years later, the wash was ten to twenty-five feet deep.

Grazing is now more closely monitored and regulated, but the ecological damage may never be repaired. Some plant communities may have been irrevocably altered by the elimination of certain species of plants.

While national attention has been focused on the raging controversy over cutting versus saving old growth forest in the Pacific Northwest, timber harvesting of ancient trees has quietly continued in the Southwest.

Overmature, decadent, nonproductive. These are a few of the euphemisms used by the Forest Service and timber industry to describe old growth forest, until recently. A new forestry is emerging, at least in parts of the West. Instead of practicing what Arnold Bolle, dean emeritus of the University of Montana's Forestry School, called "Nazi forestry"—that is, clearcutting the timber and burning the rest—the new forestry directives purport to examine the health of the entire forest, not just individual trees. A directive in 1990 from the Forest Service in Washington, D.C., reads, "The national forests no longer grow trees for the sole purpose of providing wood products for the nation."

Typically, a tree living half a millennium does most of its growing in the first century. Foresters use to call this first fifth of its natural life "rotation age" and considered the other four-fifths a waste. But many studies now show that the slow maturing process is vital to the overall health of the forest. For example, the symbiotic relationship between underground fungi and tree roots needs time to develop; heavy harvesting can prevent this mutually beneficial relationship from occurring. According to botanist Jack States, "A loss of sixty percent of the canopy cover has a significant reduction on truffle productivity. Where direct sunlight hits the forest floor, truffles disappear."

Surprisingly, even downed deadwood and standing snags play an important role in the forest's ecosystem. At one time foresters believed that snags attracted lightning, thus the dead trees should be removed. Today we realize that snags, which may stand for a century or more, provide shelter and food for dozens of species of wildlife. Once the tree falls, it continues to decompose and enrich the soil. The new forestry is an attempt to consider the complexities and value of the forest ecosystem and determine a level of logging that won't destroy the forest's richness. Foresters warn that research has only scratched the surface in providing the information needed to make wise decisions.

Occasionally, managerial decisions that were in the past considered "biologically correct" have been shown to be false or improperly applied in the field. One example has been the management goal of increasing biological diversity through logging practices that increase "edge effect."

Wildlife biologists have noticed that where two distinct habitats meet, the interface, or edge, is often richer in the number of species it supports than either of the two adjoining habitats alone. Edges may contain the species from both habitats as well as species and hybrids specialized to edges. As ecologists such as Thomas Whitham have pointed out, "plant hybrid zones are hot spots of ecological and evolutionary activity and should be conserved."

Unfortunately, land managers were sometimes misled into thinking that simply increasing the amount of edge would be beneficial to the entire ecosystem. For instance, creating more forest-meadow edge could be achieved by cutting swaths through the forest, thus rationalizing more timber harvesting. However, when overapplied, the result is fragments or islands of forest that are too small for those plants and animals that require relatively large undisturbed habitats for survival. Also, the lack of vegetative cover between islands prevents movement of many animals between them. Additionally, artificially created edges usually attract "weedy" species,

Large, mature ponderosa pines like these in the Pine Flat Campground in upper Oak Creek Canyon are found scattered throughout the forest, but few virgin stands of old growth remain. Much of the Coconino National Forest is already second- growth forest.

In 1920 the largest Arizona ponderosa was cut on the Coconino National Forest. It was a behemoth: six feet across forty feet up from its base and 640 years old.

those that are already quite common elsewhere. What was thought to be good for increasing natural biodiversity only disrupts the native ecosystem.

The number of species or habitats alone is a poor criterion for conservation. Striving for biodiversity can lead managers to over-manipulate areas. A better goal is a full complement of native species living in natural patterns of abundance. This is not an easy or simple task in light of our rudimentary understanding of the complex relationships of the various forest plants and animals, and the ever-increasing economic and recreational demands being placed on the forest.

On the Coconino National Forest surrounding the Red Rock–Sacred Mountain region, the new forestry initiative has not yet been wholly embraced. While individual foresters strive for a better ecologically balanced forest, bureaucratic and political forces often take precedence. Of concern to many is whether forests dominated by young managed stands will perform the same ecological functions as old growth forests such as providing nesting sites for cavity-nesting birds and mammals.

John Nelson says, "Until about five years ago, the Coconino used the 'pick and pluck' method of harvesting, that is, selective cutting, taking one tree here and another over there and leaving a few in between. Lately, even-age management has come in which has resulted in heavier cuts and the long-range goal of changing the natural diversity of the forest to uniform stands of even-aged trees [trees all the same age]." This style of cutting has also increased fragmentation of the forest into smaller and smaller pieces.

This heavier harvesting has adversely affected many of the forest's residents, including the black bear. Al Le-Count, a research biologist with the Arizona Game and Fish Department, has studied Arizona bears for over sixteen years. He believes that black bears probably never were very common in the ponderosa pine forest around Flagstaff; he estimates that there is about one bear per six to ten square miles. However, in mixed conifer forest, which in this area is limited to drainages and some of the higher mountain slopes, and in the dense chaparral at lower elevations, bear density can be as high as one per square mile. Why the difference?

LeCount has learned that the biggest factor is the density of vegetation between one to six feet above the ground. Black bears apparently relish their privacy and therefore require enough screening so they are hidden from view at particular distances.

In the case of open ponderosa pine forest, there may be only 8 percent cover from one to six feet above the ground, and a bear can be seen from nearly a hundred feet away. In mixed conifer, the cover increases to 34 percent and the "sight distance" drops to about fifty feet. Old growth chaparral is extremely thick and a bear may be hidden from view in just a few feet.

Usually the mixed conifer stands and the chaparral occur on steep slopes, another favorite haunt of the bear. For feeding or to travel from one area to the next (males will range up to 150 square miles), black bears follow drainages or corridors of thick vegetation. Therefore, Le-Count has been recommending that timber harvesting be done in such a manner as to not only preserve mixed conifer stands and chaparral but also to keep pathways between stands so bears do not become isolated from each other.

LeCount also discovered that mother bears use big, old pines as baby-sitters. She encourages the cubs to climb high into a tree. Then she can forage, knowing her babies are out of harm's way.

Although black bears have many of the same habitat requirements that other old growth species need, the forest managers paid little attention to LeCount's recommendations; that is, until a tiny owl caught the public eye.

One of three subspecies of spotted owls, the Mexican spotted owl, is distributed through coniferous forests from the Sinaloa mountains in western Mexico north to Arizona and New Mexico, southern Colorado, southern Utah, and extreme western Texas. The spotted owl has deep brown eyes, one of the few dark-eyed owls in North America. The adults are from sixteen to eighteen inches high and have a wingspan of about four feet. They eat bats, insects, other small owls, and rodents.

A new moon in September is one of the very best times to hear spotted owls calling. Bugling elk seem to provoke the owls into being boisterous. If you imitate the spotted owl's hooting, not only may an aggressive owl fly in to investigate, but a coyote may also wander by to check you out.

When biologist Joe Ganey began his research on the Mexican spotted owl several years ago, he determined that in northern Arizona mixed-conifer forests of uneven-aged trees dominated by Douglas fir and/or white fir with a prominent pine component were a preferred habitat for the spotted owl. Continuing studies, headed by wildlife biologist Cecelia Dargan of the Forest Service, indicate that old growth ponderosa mixed with Gambel oak appears to be another important spotted owl habitat. Additionally, some lightly logged areas that have young ponderosa pines and enough shrubby understory to mimic the vertical structure and cover of old growth also contain owls.

So far, 114 owl territories have been discovered on the Coconino National Forest; scientists estimate that this probably represents 80 percent of the total. The majority of these territories contain a pair of owls; the remaining territories have a single individual. The owl territories are concentrated in the San Francisco Peaks–Mount Elden area, along the Mogollon Rim, and in the deep canyons between Oak Creek and Sycamore. A clustering of territories in the Mormon Mountain–Hutch Mountain area in the central part of the forest delighted the biologists who felt that these owl centers were close enough to each other that individual owls could fly between them – a necessity to mixing the gene pool and maintaining the viability of the population.

Unfortunately, of the known owl territories on the Coconino National Forest, about two-thirds of the nests are located within active or planned timber sales or forest lands that may be harvested in the future. Only one third of the nests are on reserved land such as designated wilderness.

The Forest Service considers the owl to be a "sensitive species," and therefore gives it special consideration. Each pair of owls uses about two thousand acres of forest as its home range. On average, half of that acreage is old growth forest. The fallen logs in the uncut areas provide habitat for the small mammals such as deer mice, wood rats, and voles that comprise the bulk of the owls' diet. Mexican spotted owls also seem to require the shade and resulting coolness provided by denser forest lots. If an owl nest is located within a timber sale, a circle with a radius of about one-half mile and the nest at the center is reserved as a protected area. An additional buffer zone of 1,550 acres (the approximate amount of territory needed for foraging) is restricted in terms of logging.

During 1992, the U.S. Fish and Wildlife Service will be holding hearings across the Southwest to decide whether to list the Mexican spotted owl as a threatened or endangered species. Depending upon whose definition is used for old growth, approximately 75 percent of the presettlement old growth of the Southwest has already been logged and many owl biologists believe the Mexican spotted owl is in danger of extirpation in Arizona and New Mexico. Conservationists find the hearings ironic since threatened or endangered species status should be based solely on scientific facts, not public opinion.

Another "sensitive" resident of old growth ponderosa pine forests is the northern goshawk. The goshawk's diet consists of roughly equal amounts of birds and mammals, with Abert squirrels making up more than half of the mammal portion. The goshawk prefers to nest in stands of dense, large trees where the canopy interlocks, not

Above: Where and how much to log remains a controversial subject around Flagstaff. Right: Over the past fifty years, northern goshawk populations have plummeted in northern Arizona. The exact cause of this decline is hotly debated but most studies indicate a definite relationship between loss of nesting goshawks and loss of old growth forests. (Photo copyright by Noel and Helen Snyder)

78

unlike the Abert squirrel. These birds tend to reoccupy the same nest tree year after year. An ongoing survey as of September, 1991, had located 137 pairs of goshawks in Arizona.

The U.S. Fish and Wildlife Service has not yet recommended the goshawk for threatened or endangered status. Nonetheless, the Forest Service is currently protecting a thirty-acre core around each nest where no logging may take place. A six-hundred-acre post-fledgling area can be lightly harvested and a six-thousand-acre foraging area may also be subject to limited cutting. These regulations will be up for review in 1992.

No studies of the effects of timber harvesting on goshawks have been conducted on the Coconino National Forest; however, research has been done on the nearby North Kaibab National Forest. In spite of thirty-acre, no-cut buffer zones around nests on the North Kaibab, goshawk populations have plummeted over the years—from 260 goshawk pairs in the 1940s to sixty pairs in 1988 and forty pairs in 1989. A study funded by the timber industry attributed the decline to natural fluctuations in prey populations. However, other studies do not bear this out since similar declines were *not* noted in control (non-harvested) plots.

Occasionally, other raptors, such as red-tailed hawks, great horned owls, and Cooper's hawks, have replaced the goshawks in logged areas. Managers are faced with the dilemma of choosing different prescriptions while knowing that certain species of wildlife may be adversely affected but some species may actually increase. Science is of little help in these tough value judgments.

Still, the diversity of old growth makes a strong case for its existence. Sam Hitt, president of Forest Guardians, a Santa Fe–based group, states that the goshawk serves as an indicator species for one hundred to three hundred other potentially threatened plant and animal species in old growth.

While extinction of only one species may not be perceived as a terrible loss, remember the analogy of a flying airplane losing a rivet. One rivet may not matter, two may not cause any concern, but keep popping rivets and at some point the airplane falls apart and crashes. The diversity of life in the forest and other ecosystems is the product of the continuing natural experiment called evolution. The land managers need to remember Aldo Leopold's suggestion: "The first rule of intelligent tinkering is to save all the pieces." The Endangered Species Act is one of our best tools for saving all the pieces; however, the act itself is endangered since it comes up for review as this book goes to press (1992).

The greatest value of old growth does not lie in its economic worth but in the removal of carbon dioxide from the atmosphere and its replacement with oxygen, the maintenance of the watershed and topsoil, and the survival of dependent species, which contributes to genetic diversity that probably buffers against ecological catastrophe. And the health of the forest is not based on the survival of just one species but the whole complement of plants and animals interrelating.

With almost all the big yellow pines gone, most timber companies still seem to practice an "economy of extinction" rather than an "economy of sustainability." As T. H. Watkins, editor of *Wilderness,* warns, "Lumber companies are not in the forest business; they are in the tree business." Their main concern seems to be to cut their financial losses as much as possible and to try to shift the blame for their situation away from their management practices to make the environmentalist a scapegoat.

In the end, the issue of saving old growth is really an issue of maintaining an ecologically healthy and diverse forest—a forest that can continually renew itself through time and provide food and shelter not only for its indigenous plants and animals but for humankind as well. Forest managers, timber people, and environmentalists have a most difficult challenge before them.

Above left: Of the over one hundred Mexican spotted owl breeding territories known in the Red Rock–Sacred Mountain area, only about a third of the nests are on reserved land such as designated wilderness. The remaining two-thirds are located within active or planned timber sales or forest lands that may be harvested in the future. (Photo courtesy of the Coconino National Forest) Above right: The oldest ponderosa pine ever recorded was 1,047 years old when it was felled in the early 1900s in Colorado. More typically the pines grow to be 350 to 500 years old before succumbing to disease or fire. Below: In the open ponderosa pine forest around Flagstaff, black bears are not very common—there is perhaps one bear in every six to ten miles. However, in mixed conifer forest (which in the Red Rock–Sacred Mountain region is limited to drainages and some of the higher mountain slopes) and in the dense chaparral-type vegetation in the canyons along the Mogollon Rim, bear densities may be as high as one per square mile. Apparently, black bears relish their privacy and require a certain density of vegetation between one and six feet above the ground as provided by old growth stands of mixed conifers and chaparral.

THE RIPARIAN WAY

UPPER LAKE MARY. At first I thought a small bald eagle was sitting in the pine snag. Bald eagles are not uncommon migrants along the Mogollon Rim, especially near lakes; fifty to seventy-five eagles overwinter in the Verde Valley. Years ago, a pair of eagles nested by Foxboro Lake in the pine forest south of Flagstaff, so spotting an eagle here is not impossible. As my wife Ann and I paddled the kayak closer, we could see that the snowy white color on the head continued down the breast to the legs— definitely a fish hawk or osprey, not an eagle. I prefer the old name fish hawk because it is so apropos. The bird is equipped with unusually long talons, a reversible fourth (outer) toe, and spines on the soles of its feet, all adaptations for grasping slippery, struggling fish, its main prey. Osprey, the common name considered official by the

American Ornithologist's Union, comes from a series of not very interesting errors and corruptions of *ossifraga,* or "bone crusher," a term most aptly applied to an Old World marrow-eating vulture, which resembles the osprey not at all.

The osprey is a cosmopolitan species but fairly restricted in the American Southwest, where its main food is obviously limited by a dearth of permanent lakes and streams. Though the osprey was uncommon to start with, during the 1950s and 1960s fish and game rangers were instructed to shoot the bird on sight in a misguided attempt to improve Arizona's game fishery. Furthermore, during the 1960s, North American osprey populations suffered a serious decline because of the indiscriminate use of chlorinated hydrocarbon pesticides, particularly

DDT. These highly toxic, long-lasting chemicals washed into rivers and lakes and became concentrated in the tissues of fish. Once ingested by birds, the DDT caused their egg shells to be exceptionally thin, thus susceptible to cracking during incubation. Since the banning of DDT in the United States in 1972, fish-eating raptors have made a comeback. (Deplorably, these dangerous pesticides are still manufactured in the U.S. and elsewhere and exported to other countries.)

From April to August, ospreys may be seen at Upper Lake Mary, Mormon Lake, Marshall Lake, and Ashurst Lake. One nest is located in Newman Canyon Cove on the south side of Upper Lake Mary. The original osprey nesting site was damaged by a wind storm so the Forest Service, Arizona Game and Fish Department, and the Northern Arizona Audubon Society erected an artificial nesting platform. The platform has been successful, with the ospreys raising two to three young per year. Some osprey nests are used for thirty years or more.

For the osprey water is life, but water is a scarce and precious resource in the Red Rock–Sacred Mountain area. Nevertheless, it was water, or at least the promise of permanent water in an arid region, that encouraged the first non-Indian settlers.

In May of 1876, about fifty New Englanders, the first group of pioneers to attempt to settle the Flagstaff area, were led here by exaggerated tales of fertile, watered valleys. They had hoped to find good land in the Little Colorado River Valley, but discovered instead that Mormons had already claimed all the arable land there for themselves. Another lure was reports of gold only fifteen miles from the San Francisco Peaks. (Latite pipes, an extrusive igneous feature, on the western side of the White Horse Hills north of the Peaks, contain minor amounts of the iron minerals limonite and hematite, and traces of silver and gold. It is conceivable, though unlikely, that this was the source of the alleged placer deposits.)

Within several weeks, most of these men had abandoned the high country. A second "Boston Party" arrived in July and local legend has them stripping a tall ponderosa of its branches and hoisting a flag (the origin of the present name for the town) to celebrate the country's centennial. But most of these folks moved on once they discovered the lack of streams and rivers in the area. The permanent settlement of Flagstaff would be a slow, sporadic process.

Precipitation over the Red Rock–Sacred Mountain area arrives generally during two different seasons: winter and summer. Winter rains and snows result from storms brought out of the Pacific by westerly winds. Pacific storms originating to the southwest of Arizona tend to be moisture-laden and relatively warm, sometimes even bringing rain as high as the eight-thousand-foot level in mid-winter. Pacific storms born in the Gulf of Alaska occasionally sweep down to the area but typically are drier and colder air masses. When storms from both sources collide over the Southwest, the region can receive prodigious amounts of snow: One series of storms in December of 1967 left three feet in Sedona and over seven along the Mogollon Rim.

Summer precipitation is derived from a completely different source. In early summer, a stationary high pressure cell begins to build over the Gulf of Mexico. Moist air moving clockwise around this cell starts to be transported across Mexico and into the Southwest usually by sometime in July. Clear mornings are followed by afternoon thunderstorms resulting from the heating and uplifting of moist air over the Mogollon Rim and mountains. By late afternoon, cooling temperatures dissipate the clouds. These "summer monsoons" can be quite intense but are usually very localized. The Gulf of Mexico high breaks down by September and dry air returns to the Southwest.

The two "rainy" seasons do not add up to much moisture. The ponderosa pine forest averages nineteen inches of precipitation per year and the Sedona area records seventeen. (The lower elevation of Sedona and the consequently higher temperatures result in a higher evaporation rate and less moisture available for plants, thus woodland instead of forest.) Much of the moisture that falls seeps deep into porous ground, runs off quickly, evaporates, or sublimates in the case of snow, and is not available for plants and animals.

A little of this precipitation reappears as springs and a few streams such as Oak Creek and Wet Beaver below the Mogollon Rim. Permanent, year-round streams are nonexistent above the Mogollon Rim. Apparently a stream used to flow out of the Inner Basin of San Francisco Peaks. Vernon Bailey noted in 1889, "There is a nice stream of water running down it [Inner Basin] now & it is full of trees." A fire in the late 1800s destroyed the springs.

Spring run-off from melting snows are the only streams seen today around the Sacred Mountain area. A photograph of the Peaks taken by Jack Hillers in 1872 shows a cienega (wet meadow) of Bebb willows (*Salix bebbiana*) and marsh plants, substantial amounts of herbaceous vegetation with occasional aspens and corridors of pines and other conifers. A hundred years later the cienega is gone, along with much of the herbaceous growth. There are many more aspens and conifers. Only

A heavy winter snowpack usually results in lavish displays of spring wildflowers like these evening-primroses (Oenothera sp.) near Flagstaff.

a small stand of Bebb willows survive in a drainage in Hart Prairie high on the western slope of the Peaks. Scientists speculate on the cause for the change: overgrazing, fire suppression, climatic change?

The high country contains few lakes. Those that do exist are shallow and small, occasionally drying up during a long summer. Chorus frogs and tiger salamanders breed in these ponds.

When the summer rains come, Arizona treefrogs emerge from underground and migrate toward the ephemeral rain pools, especially large, grassy, shallow ones at the edge of an open park or meadow. The males sing a low-pitched, harsh, metallic clack, hardly pleasing to the human ear but apparently irresistibly romantic to a female treefrog. Adaptive camouflage and clever ventriloquism aid the frog in escaping detection by predators.

As a female hops by, a male jumps on her and locks into the amphibian embrace known as amplexus. While she begins squeezing out pin-head size eggs, the male fertilizes the emerging mass. When about a small teacup-sized clump of eggs is laid, they are attached to grass stems just below the surface of the water. The love-spent frogs climb into a pine tree, ascend seventy feet or more, and feed on bark beetles and other invertebrates.

If all goes well, the eggs hatch into tadpoles and the tadpoles metamorphose into frogs before the pool dries up.

Mormon Lake, southeast of Flagstaff, is Arizona's largest "natural" lake. (Lake Mary was created in 1903 by damming the drainages feeding Walnut Creek. An additional dam in the 1940s formed Upper Lake Mary, which is a major source of drinking water for Flagstaff.) Before the nineteenth century, it was a wet-weather lake, filling after heavy rains or with the runoff from melting snows and then draining. In 1878, when sandhill cranes still frequented the marshy valley, Mormons established a dairy on the west side of the lake. The hundred or so dairy cows that grazed the large wet meadow eventually compacted the soil, clogging the natural drainage channels, and water began to collect. Eventually a lake four miles long by three miles wide and less than six feet in depth formed. The lake disappeared in 1947 during a drought period that lasted until the early 1960s. And while the lake has held perennial water over the last thirty years, several years of recent drought have substantially reduced its size.

On a late summer day, near the lake's shore, a great blue heron is quietly, slowly stalking fish fry. In the mud flat, white-faced ibis probe the muck with their long, gracefully curved bills; it's a scene more reminiscent of the Nile in Egypt than the American Southwest. Coots or mudhens paddle and bob amongst the smartweed,

waterweed, and bulrush, where an occasional yellow-headed blackbird "sings" a cacophonous strangling noise. An elegant western grebe surfaces after a fishing dive. Perhaps a female grebe is nearby carrying the young ones on her back.

On shore, note the ubiquitous robin, the green-backed variety of the lesser goldfinch, a lone Townsend's solitaire calling its single note, a raucous flock of crows, a black-headed grosbeak, and a brightly attired male western tanager—all relishing ripening berries.

Already in fruit are black walnuts, currants, wild grapes, squawbush berries, Utah serviceberries, elderberries, and Arizona rosehips. Birds, gray-collared chipmunks, rock squirrels, and several humans compete for nature's bounty.

Anglers of all ages are fishing for bullhead catfish and northern pike. However, in a few weeks, they will be succeeded by duck hunters here and at the small lakes and ponds scattered about Anderson Mesa. Mallards, pintails, cinnamon teal, redheads, and ruddy ducks will have completed their nesting and begin migrating through the area.

Besides the lakes and ponds, streams provide important wildlife habitat. Without a doubt, Oak Creek is the most significant permanent water course running through the Red Rock–Sacred Mountain area. From a fractured section of Coconino Sandstone, water bubbles up from the earth to form one of the most delightful trout streams in Arizona. The upper creek supports a lush riparian (streamside) habitat of New Mexico alder, box elder, bigtooth maple, narrowleaf cottonwood, and velvet ash. Ponderosa pine, Douglas fir, white fir, and spruce can also be found. Coffeeberry, red willow, arroyo willow, Arizona rose, wild grape, Virginia creeper, New Mexico raspberry, Himalaya berry, and red raspberry form a dense undergrowth. Giant horsetails, scouring rush, river sedge, beebalm and other mints, watercress, and yellow monkeyflower cover the muddy banks or grow in tight clumps on islands of soil in the stream.

Downstream there is a subtle change in the plant growth. Arizona sycamore, Fremont cottonwood, and Arizona walnut become the dominant trees. New Mexico alder continues to occur but only in scattered dense stands. The understory is reduced considerably although grape, Virginia creeper, and most of the sedges and tall grasses remain. Nearing Sedona, mesquite, catclaw acacia, and seep willow make their appearance.

Of the over 250 species of amphibians, reptiles, mammals, and birds that inhabit the Red Rock Country, 50 percent or more utilize the riparian areas at some time during the year or their life cycle. Of these 125 or so species,

Streams flowing off the Mogollon Rim, some permanent and others intermittent, have carved numerous deep canyons. Some of the gorges contain the last vestiges of riparian habitats in the Red Rock–Sacred Mountain area.

Above: Cranesbill geranium (Geranium caespitosum) is one of many perennial wildflowers that depend upon moist habitats, such as stream banks, for survival. Left: When the summer rains come, Arizona treefrogs (Hyla wrightorum) emerge from underground, breed in the ephemeral rain pools, and then climb in ponderosa pines to feed on bark beetles and other invertebrates.

about 60 percent (approximately seventy-five species) require the riparian areas for survival and/or reproduction. Another 30 percent occasionally use the riparian zone.

As recently as a hundred years ago, many of Arizona's dry desert washes and intermittent streams were permanent water courses lined with stately cottonwoods, huge mesquite trees, and other lush vegetation. These rivers and streams formed green chains of life through the forbidding desert country, but according to wildlife biologist Mary Gilbert of the Verde Ranger District, 95 percent of Arizona's riparian habitat has been destroyed.

Livestock grazing in the late nineteenth century had a profound effect upon the native vegetation. Huge herds of cattle, horses, sheep, and goats quickly overgrazed vast areas of Arizona. Nature conspired with the ranchers in that the Southwest's rainfall pattern began to change around the turn of the century. Instead of moisture coming as gentle springtime rains, the initial growing season was left hot and dry. When the rains finally did arrive in July and August, they often came as short but violent thundershowers. The fragile desert soil laid bare by overgrazing was washed away in flashfloods. Aquifers were destroyed, springs silted in, and many rivers and streams became intermittent or dried up entirely. To add insult to injury, the rivers were often subjected to damming and channelizing. Any remaining riparian vegetation was occasionally managed to near extinction. For instance, during the 1960s, the Salt River Project, a Phoenix-based utility company, attempted to cut five of every six mature cottonwood trees on private land along the Verde River to increase runoff. The company felt that the trees used too much of the water.

Studies done by biologists Steve Carothers, Roy Johnson, and others have shown that the Verde River and its tributary riparian communities were some of the richest for non-colonial nesting birds in the state, perhaps the richest in North America. In 1971 as many 847 pairs of birds, representing twenty-six different species, were breeding per one hundred acres of Verde riparian habitat. These extremely high densities were partly possible because adjacent agricultural lands provided a very high density of insect food for the birds. But even on riparian sites away from the farms, along Oak Creek, Dry Beaver Creek, and West Clear Creek, breeding bird densities still ranged from two hundred to over 350 pairs per one hun-

dred acres. In comparison, an average Eastern deciduous forest supports about two hundred pairs per one hundred acres and open desert between zero and thirty-seven pairs per one hundred acres. Although Salt River Project's plan was scrapped, local residents along the Verde River have removed many trees, further degrading the habitat.

Riparian habitats provide more than just nest sites for birds. The vegetation helps slow down flood waters, and the roots hold the banks together, stemming erosion and providing a "sponge" that absorbs water that can be released at low stream levels. The overhanging branches shade the stream from the desert sun and help keep the water temperature lower. A cooler stream can hold more oxygen for fish and other organisms and decaying leaves release nutrients for plankton, which form the basis of the aquatic food chain. Between 50 and 70 percent of the energy for producing fish comes from land vegetation.

The Arizona Game and Fish Department has designated a number of the Red Rock Country riparian animals as Threatened Species. Included on their list are: bald eagle, willow flycatcher, osprey, yellow-billed cuckoo, common blackhawk, peregrine falcon, belted kingfisher, Mexican gartersnake, lowland leopard frog, red bat, spikedace, roundtail chub, razorback sucker, and Colorado River squawfish. Other riparian animals of concern are the hognosed skunk, hooded skunk, river otter, and the very rare silver-haired bat.

The spikedace, a tiny silvery minnow, is listed by the U.S. Fish and Wildlife Service as an Endangered Species and may help protect the environment of the upper Verde River. Protecting obscure species opens conservationists to ridicule by those who do not understand the importance of saving habitats by saving all the pieces. Since there is no federal law to protect endangered habitats, the Endangered Species Act is the best tool conservationists have to save what little is left.

It's very easy to take water for granted. Turn on the faucet and out it comes. But if there is one primary limiting factor to survival in the Southwest, it is water. Here in the land of the Sierra de Sin Agua, we must always remember how precious a gift water is, learn to conserve it, and protect our sources of water through better management of our natural resources. Not only will the wildlife be thankful, but our continued existence in the Southwest demands it.

Above: Spring run-off from melting snows are just about the only flowing streams seen today around the Sacred Mountain area. Left: Oak Creek Canyon is probably the most important riparian habitat in the Red Rock–Sacred Mountain area. Right: At higher elevations (above six thousand feet), about half of the annual precipitation comes in the form of snow.

The riparian community along Oak Creek is actually a series of overlapping plant communities that require an abundant and dependable water source. More than half of the 250 species of amphibians, reptiles, mammals, and birds that inhabit the Red Rock Country utilize riparian habitats at some time during the year or their life cycle. Inset: A few plant species are found only in limited geographic areas. One of these endemics is Arizona bugbane (Cimicifuga arizonica) which grows only in wooded ravines in the Red Rock–Sacred Mountain area.

90

A plant of rich, moist soils in coniferous forests, this is the only species of cinquefoil (Potentilla thurberi) in the area that has deep red flowers.

Above: In this arid region, monkeyflowers (Mimulus sp.) are found only in riparian habitats or in hanging gardens watered by seeps on cliffs. Right: Cathedral Rock, seen from Red Rock Crossing on lower Oak Creek.

PYGMY FORESTS

I SWING THE AX hard and the log splits with a decisive crack. The shaggy bark sloughs off revealing a maze of insect galleries chewed into the sapwood. The cedarlike smell drifts upward. I feel a bit guilty knowing that junipers can live for more than a thousand years. But I also know that these particular trees were from a pygmy forest destined to be thinned by the Forest Service.

The first time I heard the phrase "pygmy forest" I envisioned dwarf natives stalking midget deer. I was subsequently informed that the label referred to the diminutive nature of the trees, not to the forest's other inhabitants.

The pygmy forest is also known as the pinyon pine–juniper woodland, or simply PJ. Extensive areas of the Intermountain West are covered in PJ, and the Red Rock–Sacred Mountain area is no exception. In places that are too hot and dry for ponderosa pine but still more hospitable than desert, pinyon pines and several species of juniper grow. Within the woodland, there are definite spatial differences in which species and how many of each type of tree will occur. The pinyons tend to be at the more moist locations (which are often directly related to higher elevations or northern exposures) and the junipers tend to be in the drier spots.

The pinyon pine (*Pinus edulis*) is a short-needled pine; the needles average an inch and a half in length, and when first born appear as a single blade that later splits into two. A close relative, the single-leaf pinyon (*Pinus monophylla*), is irregularly found below the Mogollon Rim. The two species may interbreed, and both produce a tasty, nutritious nut that has been highly prized by Native

Americans for thousands of years and today commands exorbitant prices at the grocery market.

The pine nut's appeal is easy to understand once you have tasted one. Scientific analysis reveals that the nut meat is approximately 14 percent protein, 65 percent fat, and 18 percent carbohydrates. One pound of shelled nuts yields 2,880, calories which exceeds a pound of chocolate. The biological value of the protein approaches that of beef steak. All twenty known amino acids, the building blocks of protein, are found in the nuts; nine of these acids are essential to human growth. Additionally, the nuts are rich in phosphorous and iron and contain significant amounts of vitamin A, thiamine, riboflavin, and niacin. Statistics aside, the nut simply tastes good.

Members of the corvid family would seem to agree. Four species, Clark's nutcracker, scrub jay, Steller's jay, and pinyon jay, are known to eat and cache pine seeds.

Beginning in late summer, flocks of pinyon jays peck loose ripening pinyon pine cones, carry them to a safe perch, and pick them apart scale by scale. Research conducted by Russell Balda and Steve Vanderwall has revealed that up to twenty seeds are temporarily stored in the jay's elastic esophagus. The seeds are carried off to the traditional nesting area, perhaps as far as six miles, and planted in the ground. Only a fraction of the buried seeds will be utilized the following breeding season as food.

The jay's selection of seeds is not random. Viable seeds have a dark brown case; others are light tan. Good seeds weigh more than empty cases, and clicking the case with the bill differentiates full ones from empties. Thus through sight, touch, and sound, the jays quickly reject or accept seeds.

The pinyon tree benefits from this caching activity by having its seeds dispersed and planted below the surface. Pinyon pine seeds that simply fall to the ground at the base of the parent tree usually dry out and die.

Some of the PJ woodlands in Sunset Crater National Monument display natural bonsai pinyons. These exceptionally short and odd-shaped pinyons bear the marks of *Dioryctria albovitella*, a cone- and shoot-boring moth. Northern Arizona University biologists Susan Mopper and Thomas Whitham have discovered that the female moth lays an egg on a new shoot bud. A tiny larvae emerges from the egg and bores into the shoot, where it lies dormant until the following spring. At that time, the larvae begins feeding by boring into and killing a canopy branch tip or a developing female cone. After about four weeks of feeding, the larvae pupate briefly inside of a branch shoot and emerge as adults in July.

As this life cycle is repeated year after year, the canopy of the pinyons becomes permanently contorted. The larvae's feeding behavior also changes the tree's sex. Pinyons are monoecious; that is, each tree contains male and female flowers (cones). The male cones are located on the smaller, lateral branches and the female cones are on the stout terminal shoots forming the upper canopy. The moth larvae prefer to feed on the female cones, so over time the tree becomes more male!

Although infestation by these moths may seem detrimental, researcher Kerry Christensen suggests that there may be an overall positive affect on the woodland. In uninfested trees, cones, and therefore seeds, are abundantly produced in four- to seven-year cycles interspersed with years of possibly no cone production. However, in infested pinyons, the energy conserved allows low but annual cone production. This more stable food supply helps the pinyon mice, pinyon jays, Clark's nutcrackers, scrub jays, Steller's jays, plain titmice, rufous-sided towhees, and a host of other seed-eating animals. Additionally, the bonsai pinyons produce more insects that may become food for birds, and shrubby growth adds protective cover for wildlife.

The junipers of the woodlands come in four different species: alligator-bark, Rocky Mountain, Utah, and one-seed. There is a fifth species in Arizona—dwarf juniper—but it is a denizen of the montane and alpine zones and differs from the other junipers in its prostrate growth and its needlelike, rather than scalelike, leaves. The fragrant aroma of our western junipers have led cowboys, ranchers, and pioneers to call them cedars, although the botanists insist that true cedars do not occur in Arizona or for that matter in North America.

Alligator-bark and Rocky Mountain junipers are usually scattered through the transition zone between ponderosa pine forest and chaparral or between ponderosa and PJ. One glance at the deeply checkered pattern on the trunk of an alligator-bark juniper readily identifies it. This is our largest juniper, occasionally exceeding fifty feet in height.

The Rocky Mountain juniper is typically a straight-trunked tree, twenty to forty feet tall, with slender branches often drooping at the ends. It grows faster than the other junipers, making it popular as an ornamental.

Utah and one-seed junipers, with their twisted trunks covered with shaggy bark, suggest antiquity; indeed, these trees can live well over a thousand years. To distinguish these two similar species, first note their overall appearance. Utah juniper is larger (fifteen to forty feet tall),

About nine species of oaks grow in the Red Rock Country. Botanists disagree on the oaks' exact species classification status since some "species" readily interbreed with others, violating the basic definition of a species.

94

with a definite trunk, while one-seed is smaller (ten to twenty-five feet tall) and shrubby, with several branches emerging from the ground. Secondly, the former has both "berries" (actually modified female cones) and pollen-producing cones on the same tree (monoecious), while one-seed juniper comes in separate female (berries) and male (pollen) trees (dioecious).

Many ranchers and certain individuals of the Forest Service seem to regard the PJ woodland as a weedy intrusion into valuable grazing land. (To a certain extent this has happened. As desert grasslands became overgrazed and wildfires were controlled, juniper and pinyon invaded these areas.) They see the trees' only value as being raw material for making fence posts, pencils, and firewood. Large expenditures of money and countless hours of labor have been spent attempting to eradicate the woodland; although in many cases, there was little or no evidence that that particular plot of trees was a recent invader. The idea behind this scheme is that grasses will replace the woodland and thus expand the acreage available for livestock grazing. Other touted "benefits" included increased water yield through increased runoff, increased mule deer habitat, and reduced erosion.

One technique of mass destruction is to stretch a heavy-gauge anchor chain between two D-9 Caterpillars and drive through a woodland, mowing down anything and everything in their path—a process known as chaining. A custom-built eighty-ton vehicle called the Tree Crusher has also been used for a similar result.

The tree carcasses are bulldozed into piles, left to dry, and then burned. The raw earth is sown with grasses (often crested wheatgrass, a central-Asia native) deemed nutritious and tasty to cattle, horses, and sheep. Unfortunately, a typical scenario is that the tender grass shoots (which appear only if there has been enough rain to allow the seeds to germinate) are munched by too many livestock too soon and "weedy species" (meaning those flowers and shrubs that cows don't or won't eat) invade the newly created meadow. Sagebrush, snakeweed, rabbitbrush, locoweed, and globemallow are common pioneer plants in the woodlands. Given time, the resolute pinyon pines and junipers make a comeback and on a human time scale form a fairly stable climax community unless somehow disturbed again.

None of the other expected benefits have occurred as documented by the Forest Service's own studies. Furthermore, chaining has not been cost effective. Archaeologists are angry, too, because chaining effectively destroys 100 percent of the prehistoric and historic resources of the site.

As botanists have suggested, perhaps a better approach

is to examine the potential of PJ woodlands to produce high-grade vegetable protein and oil from pinyon nuts and wood products rather than as potential pasture. The woodland deserves more from us than a mechanical slap in the face.

A rather unique feature of some of the woodlands near Sedona and along the base of the Mogollon Rim are pockets of evergreen oaks and Arizona cypress.

The oaks of the Red Rock Country, like the pinyon pine and juniper, also tend to be diminutive in stature. Unlike PJ, they generally do not occur in homogenous stands but are scattered about, finding suitable homes along washes, on Oak Creek, or sometimes mixed in with the chaparral. One species, Gambel oak, is a resident primarily of the ponderosa forest.

Listing the species of oak in our area is not nearly as easy as one might expect. One time, feeling a little perverse, I collected leaves from different parts of the same oak tree. I presented these leaves to a botanist at the Museum of Northern Arizona (who shall in all fairness remain nameless) without telling him that they came from the same plant. After carefully examining each leaf, noting each one's color, size, shape, and other morphological features and checking these leaves against specimens in the herbarium, the botanist informed me that I had two species. I then proceeded to tell him the truth. He, of course, was rather chagrined but rationalized his identifications with a long discourse on the "problems with oaks" and hybridization. He also learned never to trust a zoologist bearing plants for identification.

There are about nine species of oak in the Red Rock Country. I say "about" nine because the exact number depends upon whether you are a "splitter" or a "lumper." Taxonomists, those scientists who busy themselves with trying to classify and categorize nature, can be divided into two schools of thought. One group, the splitters, look for every opportunity to separate out what they consider to be a distinct species, while the lumpers try to combine similar plants or creatures under one name. In the past, a working definition of a species was a group of individual plants or animals that could breed only with each other. A fairly simple criteria but flawed, especially with those plants (and a few animals) that have the ability to interbreed across artificial species lines.

Modern taxonomists are refining (or confusing?) the classification of organisms by examining their basic genetic material. Until the hybridizing oaks of Oak Creek receive such detailed attention, we will just have to muddle along with our "about nine" figure.

Of the nine, the Gambel oak (*Quercus gambelii*) is the

Arizona cypress in the Red Rock Country exemplifies endurance and survival. This woodland tree is believed to be a relict species from the last ice age, existing today in isolated pockets along the base of the Mogollon Rim.

only deciduous one, losing all of its leaves in the fall. This oak is usually ten to forty feet tall, although it may be short and scrubby in marginal habitats. It is commonly scattered throughout the ponderosa forest and extends into canyons where sufficient water and shade may be found. Its large, deeply lobed leaves are bigger than any other of the Southwestern oaks. In many respects, a Gambel oak resembles a stunted, crooked white oak (*Q. alba*) and may actually be a variety of that eastern species, split off from its ancestors by an accident of Pleistocene biogeography. The wood is prized by locals as firewood.

One of the most common oaks is the shrub live oak (*Q. turbinella*), sometimes called scrub oak. The "live" part of its name refers to the evergreen nature of this species. The evergreen oaks do drop old leaves in the fall but retain the younger ones. During prolonged droughts, evergreen oaks may lose most of their leaves, which helps conserve moisture.

The shrub live oak is found on the hot, dry slopes of the canyons and is an important component of the chaparral community. It usually grows as a shrub less than eight feet tall but occasionally reaches fifteen feet as a tree with an open, spreading crown. Its hollylike leaves are only one-half to one inch in length, blue-green above and yellowish green beneath. While this species and other Southwestern oaks provide browse for deer and livestock, tannin poisoning may occur in cattle if more than three-fourths of their diet consists of oak foliage. The acorns are an important food for Steller's jays, band-tailed pigeons, turkeys, and squirrels.

Another distinctive oak is the Arizona white oak (*Q. arizonica*). It is the largest of the evergreen oaks in the Red Rock Country, growing thirty to sixty feet tall. Its bark is fissured into thick light gray or whitish plates. The leaves are oblong, one to three inches long, thick and stiff, only slightly toothed, dull blue-green with sunken veins above; they are paler and densely hairy with prominent raised veins on the underside. A few of these magnificent trees grace the banks of lower Oak Creek, Dry Beaver, Dry Creek, and other drainages emptying into the Verde River.

The other six oaks (*Q. chrysolepis*, *Q. dunnii* or *palmeri*, *Q. emoryi*, *Q. grisea*, *Q. reticulata*, and *Q. undulata*) are less common or more difficult to identify because of hybridizing with their neighbors.

While oaks, like the junipers, have a visage of antiquity and sturdiness, there is yet another woodland tree in the Red Rock Country that exemplifies endurance and survival: the smooth Arizona cypress (*Cupressus arizonica*).

Cypresses have been a part of the world's flora for over fifty million years but now occupy only remnants of their former range. The thirteen species of *Cupressus* are found in a wide variety of habitats scattered in isolated populations across the Northern Hemisphere. For instance, the Monterey cypress (*Cupressus macrocarpa*) grows near sea level on northern California's Monterey Peninsula, while the giant cypress (*C. gigantea*), a tree attaining an eighteen-foot girth, grows at ten thousand feet in Tibet.

Paleobotanists (botanists who are not necessarily old but who study old plant remains) have studied fossil packrat middens that date back fifteen thousand years and more. Packrats forage no more than one hundred yards from their nests and over the years gather a fairly representative collection of the local vegetation. By identifying the plants from nests of various ages, the paleobotanists have discovered evidence for a warming and drying trend in our climate over the last ten thousand years. The Arizona cypress in particular has disappeared over much of its former range. Only relict populations exist today.

In the Red Rock–Sacred Mountain area, the Arizona cypress woodland has been reduced to isolated pockets along the base of the Mogollon Rim. In 1973, the Forest Service designated 565 acres of Casner Canyon where it joins Oak Creek Canyon as a Research Natural Area in order to preserve a representative stand of cypress.

The cypress is not alone in its dogged refusal to accept nature's global warming (as opposed to the alleged human-caused warming). Red osier dogwood (*Cornus stolonifera*), osha (*Ligusticum porteri*), Douglas fir (*Pseudotsuga menziesii*), white fir (*Abies concolor*), bigtooth maple (*Acer grandidentatum*), hophornbeam (*Ostrya knowltoni*), and other plants are now "stranded" within an arid region as disjunct or relict populations from the Pleistocene.

Relicts are not limited to plants. Possible animal relicts include the narrow-headed gartersnake (*Thamnophis rufipunctatus*), desert-grassland whiptail lizard (*Cnemidophorus uniparens*), Arizona treefrog (*Hyla wrightorum*), and southwestern toad (*Bufo microscaphus*). The Arizona gray squirrel (*Sciurus arizonensis*) may also be a refugee since it is found only in the riparian woodlands along Oak Creek, a few other drainages along the Mogollon Rim, and several other isolated riparian habitats in central and southern Arizona. In a broad sense, these riparian zones are relictual habitats.

Although not as intimidating as an ice age mammoth or saber-tooth tiger, the squirrel does nonetheless exhibit a remarkably sturdy jaw. The Arizona gray relishes acorns, the tough-shelled, inch-diameter cone of the cypress (which contains about one hundred seeds), and especially Arizona black walnuts. Anyone who has tried to crack open a black walnut can appreciate the squirrel's difficult

Above: A common but rarely seen denizen of the woodland is the tarantula. Unless roughly handled, these large spiders pose little danger to humans. Right: Manzanita is a common shrub in the pinyon pine–juniper woodland of the Red Rock Country.

task. The squirrel's relatively massive "nutcracker" mandible is not only necessary but perhaps is an example of co-evolution between plant and animal. The trees that produced thicker and tougher covered nuts that could not be eaten survived. Squirrels with relatively heavier jaws and stronger muscles could break open hard nuts and cones while their weaker siblings starved. Over countless generations, the course of evolution has been steered by the interplay of squirrel and plant.

The woodland trees have also played a role in the human history of the Red Rock–Sacred Mountain country. I pause from splitting juniper to admire the buff sapwood and rosey-tan heartwood. I hold in my hand a tangible link with Southwestern history. The Sinagua used the tough, rot-resistant wood in constructing their houses,

juniper berries were eaten, and shredded bark was smoked in cane cigarettes and woven into sandals. Juniper bark torches lit the prehistoric salt mine near Montezuma's Castle, and of course, juniper warmed the Sinagua's homes and cooked their food.

I worry about the future of our forests and woodlands. The interrelationships, the interdependencies, the startling complexity of the woodland ecosystems all form a tough intellectual nut to crack. Humans need wood and wood products, too. But maybe, like the Arizona gray squirrel, our relationship with the trees will eventually evolve to a symbiotic understanding and appreciation of our woodland neighbors. Instead of an arrogant attitude of mass destruction, maybe we can learn to live in peaceful co-existence with nature.

Above left: The Arizona gray squirrel may be a refugee from cooler and wetter times. As the Southwest has warmed and dried out, this species of squirrel has become restricted to the riparian woodlands along Oak Creek and a few other drainages in central and southern Arizona. Right: The Gambel oak may be a variety that was split off from its eastern white oak ancestors by an accident of Pleistocene biogeography. Above: To the Sinagua, juniper was one of the most useful plants. It provided fuel, beams for their homes, shredded bark that was woven into sandals or used as a disposable diaper; and the berries (actually modified cones) were eaten. Today the short, gnarly trees are often viewed as weeds to be removed so that more grass may grow for livestock. Overleaf: The mule deer, so-called because of its unusually large ears, in northern Arizona ranges from coniferous forest to chaparral. Breeding begins in early December with most of the mating over by mid-January; gestation is just short of seven months.

FIRE AND ICE

T HE SNOW IS FALLING quickly but quietly as we enter the upper parking lot at the Fairfield Snow Bowl on the San Francisco Peaks. My friend Bill and I are accompanied by eight novice – no, make that totally inexperienced – skiers. Somehow, we plan to set off in the gathering darkness, in a blizzard, to schuss our way down to Hart Prairie and the relative comfort of Fern Mountain Ranch, an old relay station coach stop on the stage route to the Grand Canyon.

Precious minutes of daylight are lost as we fiddle with everyone's ski bindings, a relatively simple device to clamp the toe of the boot to the ski, but also a frustrating instrument when one's fingers are cold and numb and unfamiliar with the act. Skis are on, backpacks are shouldered, and tentative, slippery steps are taken from the parking lot out

into the upper end of Hart Prairie. The sun has set, the snow-choked air turns an eerie dark purple color, and, single file, we set off blindly down the slope. Bill leads the way – several winters of caretaking at Fern Mountain Ranch have given him a sixth sense about finding his winter home in darkness and in snowstorms . . . we hope. I bring up the rear, ready to herd in the strays.

Skiing in the dark is always strange. With no visual clues for reference, I seem to be standing still except for the soft swish of my skis gliding through the powder, the wind in my face, and an occasional butterfly-in-the-stomach thrill when I drop into a dip. It is now so dark and snowing so hard that I can see only a few silhouetted skiers in front of me. We ski in silence. I'm sure many of our guests are feeling more than a little apprehensive about the situation. Flashlights are useless under such conditions since the beam reflects off the white, wet flakes and illuminates only the immediate area, not the distant scene. But Bill is following his nose. We pass an old ponderosa snag that I seem to remember; then a fence line that looks familiar. But my mind begins to wander.

I dream back to last fall, golden aspens, bugling elk, and fire.

Each autumn the Peaks blaze with fiery yellow. The changing of the quaking aspen leaves from summer's green to autumn's gold is a highly anticipated event. Although the transformation is controlled by heredity and length of daylight, each year's vagarities in weather make for a different display.

Botanists explain the quaking leaves by the fact that the flattened stem is perpendicular to the plane of the leaf surface; even the slightest breath of air sets the leaves trembling. But according to early Canadian folklore, the Cross was made of aspen wood and the tree has never stopped quaking since the crucifixion of Jesus Christ.

A couple of falls ago, my wife Ann and I followed the Hart Prairie Road to a particularly fine stand of white-barked quakies with golden leaves barely tinged orange—not brown, which can happen when an early frost hits. The autumn air was bracing. We walked through the grove on an old road now closed to vehicles to protect critical elk habitat.

Many of the tree trunks are scarred where elk have raked their lower incisors up and across the bark to reach sap or to eat the aspen bark. Some of the oval black scars are fresh, but a few seem to be quite old, perhaps dating back to the days of the native Merriam's elk.

By the turn of the century, overhunting and competition with livestock had proved disastrous for many animals including the native elk. The indigenous elk vanished from Arizona's forests during the first decade of this century. Early biologists considered it a separate species, Merriam's elk, named after pioneer ecologist Clinton Hart Merriam. This elk was described as having a darker nose, more reddish fur on its head and legs, a more massive skull with broader nasals, plus a few other anatomical differences from the typical American elk, or wapiti. Modern taxonomists have decided that Merriam's elk was not an independent species but rather a subspecies of the American elk. Either classification in no way lessens the tragedy that a unique animal is gone forever.

In 1913, sixty to seventy elk from Yellowstone National Park were liberated on the Sitgreaves National Forest on the north slopes of the Mogollon Plateau. Additional releases, as well as regulated hunting, have allowed the introduced elk to prosper and spread out along the Mogollon Plateau, the San Francisco Peaks, the South Rim of the Grand Canyon, and the Hualapai Mountains.

Unfortunately, new ecological problems have been created. Burgeoning elk herds browse heavily on young aspen, preventing new groves from becoming established. (Some forest rangers suggest that fire control has had a greater limiting impact on aspen regeneration than elk browsing. Also, there is some evidence that aspen seed germination was greater in the past, and that some of today's groves are genetic clones of these "ice age" trees.) Thus the Forest Service has begun to place temporary elk-proof fences around some young aspen groves until the trees are large enough to withstand browsing. Ranchers are also complaining that the numerous elk are out-competing their cattle for food. And in 1988, the Arizona Game and Fish Commission decided to permit a larger number of elk to be taken by hunters than in previous seasons. However, in 1991 the Fund for Animals, an animal rights group, succeeded in having a special hunt aborted that was aimed at thinning a local resident herd.

The aspen grove is born of fire. Above an altitude of eight thousand feet, after a hot forest fire has consumed a stand of conifers, the new opening in the forest is invaded by grasses, wildflowers, and later, shrubs. Soon a few aspen seeds germinate and send up shoots. From these infant trees roots travel out and send up more sprouts. Eventually a grove of genetically identical clones is established. Pocket gophers in an adjacent meadow may eat aspen roots and prevent the trees from invading certain open areas. The maturing aspens release chemicals that inhibit further suckering. In the shade of the grove, firs and spruce may germinate and, in two hundred to four hundred years, reach above the aspens and shade them out. The cycle is complete and the stage set for the next fire.

We pass from the aspen grove into a gorgeous meadow, where the "skeletons" of last summer's elk gentian stand tall above the golden bunch grasses. Already fresh gopher mounds snake here and there. A western bluebird lands on a sunflower stalk and several dark-eyed juncos flash their white outer tail feathers as they dive for cover. Hidden in the nearby stand of Engelmann spruce and Douglas fir, a red squirrel gives a scolding bark. Suddenly, I'm falling.

I'm falling back to the present and I catch myself before doing a face-plant in a snowdrift.

What usually takes Bill or me less than a half-hour to ski drags on to forty-five minutes, then an hour, then another thirty minutes. Have we missed the cabin? I know that we are going slow to accommodate these beginners

Rime may coat trees and rocks when supercooled clouds or fog pass over them.

but. . . . Just when panic is beginning to rear its ugly head, I hear shouts of joy. The cabin is in sight. See? Nothing to it. Wild Bill has gotten us here safely.

We unclamp our skis, stamp our boots on the front porch, and brush some of the snow from our clothes. Once inside, in the pale yellow light of a gas lantern, I can see the ice-encrusted eyelashes and beards of our group. We look like veteran arctic explorers. The kitchen woodstove is fired up and the logs in the fireplace reluctantly begin to burn. Yukon Jack and schnapps appear and happy voices break the chill night.

The next morning dawns bright, clear, and cold. The snow squeaks under my boots as I make a mad dash for the outhouse. It's going to be a great day.

After too many sourdough pancakes, we clamp into our skis for a little ski instruction from Bill before heading out on a tour. While the troops practice kicking and gliding, step turns, and kick turns, I dig a pit into the snowpack. Five and a half feet down I finally hit the dirt. The exposed profile of snow is a record of storms alternating with clear spells. The top eight inches of powder is from last evening's snowfall. This fluffy, unconsolidated cover lies on top of a hard suncrust from the previous several days of sunny weather. Near the bottom of the snowpack are several inches of a granular, sugarlike layer that isn't bonded together at all. This is depth hoar.

On clear, cold nights there is a net exchange of heat from the ground toward the snow surface. As this warmth moves upward, snow is vaporized, often near the ground; then that water vapor refreezes into delicate, angular crystals higher in the pack. These hoar crystals do not stick together because of their angular sides. Thus a weak layer is formed in the snow pack. On the flat, depth hoar is of interest to the skier only as the cause of occasional, sudden booming settlings of the snowpack. On a hillside, however, a skier cutting across the slope can release a slab of snow and find himself being tumbled, broken, and buried in an avalanche.

To the creatures that live in snowy country, snow accumulation rates versus the onset of bitter temperatures can mean life or death. Snow forms an insulating layer to protect plants and animals from subfreezing temperatures. To the long-tailed vole, a tiny lemminglike rodent with small ears, short tail, and black beady eyes, the formation of depth hoar is important in allowing the creature to forage for food under the snowpack.

Scarcity of food and frigid temperatures are the two major environmental factors affecting animals during winter. The indigenous species have evolved many ingenious behavioral and body adaptations to cope with winter.

Most insects in temperate regions have a hetero-dynamic life cycle; that is, the adults appear for a limited time during warm weather and pass the winter at some life stage in dormancy. Dormancy may occur at the egg stage, such as in the case of grasshoppers, crickets, katydids, cicadas, or aphids; the nymph stage, as in dragonflies and damselflies; the larva stage, as in butterflies and moths; or during adulthood, as in most true bugs and beetles.

Fish, amphibians, snakes, and lizards generally enter a dormant or torpid state as winter approaches. Usually this physiological change of lower body temperature and very slow respiration is triggered by decreasing air temperatures. This isn't always the case, however: Studies on several species of lizards have shown that they become dormant in winter even when kept at room temperature.

Typically, though, as winter approaches and the days grow cooler and shorter, the amphibians and reptiles seek out a wintering location that won't reach freezing temperatures. These hibernating sites, called hibernacula, might be an abandoned rodent burrow, decaying organic litter, or mud at the bottom of a lake or pond. Often the hibernaculum is jointly occupied by a number of individuals, sometimes not limited to members of one species. (For example, in Michigan, one hibernaculum contained sixty-two snakes representing seven species and fifteen amphibians belonging to three species.)

Although most birds migrate to warmer climes as winter approaches, some manage to survive the cold, snowy environment, and at least one species hibernates! The poor-will has been found dormant in the wild, something the Hopi have been aware of for some time, since their name for the bird translates to "old man who sleeps in winter." The poor-will's body temperature drops forty degrees below normal and the bird may stay in this state, surviving off body fat, for nearly three months. (Some species of hummingbirds may become dormant each night and return to normal at daybreak to reduce energy requirements; white-throated swifts are known to roost in a torpid state during periods of cold weather when insect food is unavailable.)

Dormancy in mammals varies greatly in intensity and duration. For black bears, hibernation means a period of reduced respiration but not a marked decrease in body temperature and only a partial loss of their powers of sensibility and locomotion. In short, don't disturb a hibernating bear.

At the other extreme, certain northern ground squirrels undergo such dramatic physiological changes that they appear to be near death. Other squirrels may periodically

Skiing along the crest of the San Francisco Peaks is a challenging way to explore the mountain.

awake from their torpid state to void body wastes and may venture out of the nest to forage. Our local squirrels fall into this second category.

The long-tailed vole avoids the extremes of winter not by hibernating but by staying beneath the snowpack. The snow protects the vole against low temperatures, wind, and as an added bonus, some predators. Unfortunately (from the vole's perspective), in the relatively warm, moist subnivian environment, carbon dioxide gas accumulates from the vole's respiration and from bacterial action on decaying vegetal matter. The gas excites the vole into digging vertical ventilation shafts. The escaping warm, vole-scented air attracts long-tailed weasels, gray foxes, and coyotes.

The coyote must hunt constantly during the winter to find enough food to survive. Drawn to a vole's ventilation shaft, the coyote uses its acute hearing to detect the location of the vole. The coyote jumps straight up and comes down with legs stiff, feet close together, plunging into the snow. A little quick digging and the wild canid has a meal. Rodents make up the bulk of their diet, but carrion is also important. Coyotes are rarely able to kill large mammals such as elk in winter because of the difficulties of stalking in deep snow. If the elk is already in a weakened condition, the coyote may be successful.

Deep snow with a frozen crust is the elk's worst enemy. Mature elk can move through forty inches of loose snow without excessive difficulty. If there is a thin crust, thirty inches is about their limit. It has been suggested that four feet of snow is the maximum that elk can travel through efficiently. Calves and older animals, of course, are limited by lesser amounts. In deep snow, elk travel single file; taking turns breaking trail. To feed, elk can push aside twelve- to eighteen-inch-deep snow with their noses and can dig through several feet.

But winter takes its toll. Toward the end of February, elk may be losing almost two pounds a day. If food is scarce, they stuff themselves with coarse woody browse and too much coniferous growth. Malnutrition results and is the principal cause of winter kill, although the animal may not die until winter is over. Ironically, the new spring plants are not very high in nutrients and the elk may actually expend more energy feeding than they can take in. Additionally, the spring growth can act as a laxative, exacerbating the starving animal's condition.

All this thought of stress and starving makes me notice that I'm tired and hungry. Time to ski back to the ranch and start making some of our famous Fern Mountain Dutch-oven enchiladas for supper.

The elk presently residing in the Red Rock–Sacred Mountain area all descended from transplanted animals native to Yellowstone. Inset: Bull elk drop their heavy antlers in April and grow a new pair by fall.

Elk rake their lower incisors up the trunk of aspens to get at the sap and to eat the bark. The lower edge of the scrape is sharply cut and the upper edge more ragged, because elk do not have upper incisors to bite off the strip of bark.

Above: In the early spring before leafing out, quaking aspens produce seed capsules in the form of catkins with many cottony seeds. Left: The transformation of aspen leaves from green to gold is a highly anticipated event each autumn.

The chalky-white bark of an aspen sharply contrasts with a dark basalt cliff.

As I execute a kick-turn, I notice a very pale pinkish cast to the snow underski. On these long, late winter days, a hardy alga may make its appearance on the older drifts. Small spherical algal cells are filled with the appropriately named substance hematochrome ("blood color"). This red pigment may help in absorbing radiant energy to keep the plant from freezing. These algal plant cells also concentrate airborne pollutants including radioactive fallout, a phenomenon discovered by a uranium prospector who inadvertently let his coffee pot boil dry while melting snow and heard his Geiger counter begin to click. Some people can detect the odor of watermelon coming from the snow algae, but it's not recommended for eating as diarrhea may result.

It's now late on Saturday night. Our guests have all turned in, but Bill and I are enjoying a little Yukon Jack over snow and joke about who will find a snow worm at the bottom of their glass. Snow worms, remarkable relatives of the ordinary garden-variety earthworm, live in snow and glacial ice in the northwest coastal mountain ranges of North America but have not been reported from our continental ranges . . . yet.

I step outside for another piece of firewood and notice a brilliant full moon rising behind the Peaks. The night air is perfectly still and penetratingly cold; the silence is almost palatable. The late winter constellations sparkle with such clarity that you can almost reach out and touch them. Off toward frozen Bismark Tank, a chorus of coyotes strikes up a tune of howls and yips.

Tonight with the mountain blanketed in snow, the natural world seems to be at rest; a time for renewal, a slower pace. But as I turn to go inside, the harsh whine of a snowmobile shatters the night.

Left: More than two hundred inches of snow may bury the San Francisco Peaks each winter. But once the snows melt, the alpine tundra supports about fifty species of vascular plants, of which about 90 percent are related to the flora of the Rocky Mountain tundra. One species, the San Francisco Peaks senecio (Senecio franciscanus) is an endemic, found nowhere else in the world. Right: Avalanches are not uncommon on the steep upper slopes of the San Francisco Peaks.

Above: A nearly full moon over the Sacred Mountain, the San Francisco Peaks, lends a sense of magic and mystery to the landscape. Left: Lightning-caused fires are a common natural occurrence in the ponderosa pine forest and help establish an open, savannalike forest. However, if the fire destroys an entire stand of pines, aspens may invade the newly created space.

A NEW AGE?

AUGUST 1987. As I stepped out of my car, a young boy ran up to me and excitedly inquired, "Are you here to catch a ride with Ashtar on the Mothership?"

"Well, ah, no, I don't think so," I stammered in reply.

He ran off toward Bell Rock, and I wondered what the hell he was talking about.

A large crowd of people was standing around on a long ledge of red sandstone jutting out from the base of Bell Rock, one of the more recognizable buttes of the Red Rock Country and, according to some New Agers, the site of a mystical energy vortex.

In the center of the crowd, a dozen or so people formed a circle and held hands. This was part of the ceremonies taking place today, the Harmonic Convergence, when the alignment of certain planets and forces from beyond would enlighten us deprived, soul-searching earthlings and herald a new age for humankind.

I didn't quite understand if this enlightenment was going to emanate from the vortex or if an alien spacecraft, the Mothership, was going to deliver the message. Local residents and believers had estimated throngs of thousands would attend this historic event. This was something I didn't want to miss.

All day long, a dozen or so true believers practiced their rites, but most of the crowd seemed to consist of spectators and sceptics like myself.

As the day came to a close, people drifted away. Unfortunately I didn't get carried off by a UFO or struck by lightning, nor did I learn the meaning of life. But it had been a pleasant summer day in the Red Rock Country.

Regardless of your religious beliefs, the Red Rock–Sacred Mountain area inspires. Yavapai-Apache still conduct solemn ceremonies in Boynton Canyon and Montezuma Well. At least one old medicine woman from the Huichol tribe, who live in the Sierra Madre of Mexico, continues to make an annual religious pilgrimage to the Red Rock Country. Hopi and Navajo elders climb the San Francisco Peaks to reach ancient shrines.

Many of us who live here or come on a vacation find solace and spiritual renewal while hiking a wilderness trail or fishing in Oak Creek or simply sitting at a magnificent overlook.

Most of this provocative country is in the public domain, administered by the Forest Service under a multiple-use policy. This seemingly altruistic approach espouses a variety of uses on the public land – recreation, livestock grazing, mining, timber harvesting, and wildlife habitat. But can the forest be all things to all people? Don't many of these activities conflict with each other? How can the hiker find solitude when the buzz of a chainsaw fills the forest? Or do you dare drink from a stream while a cow stands mid-calf (no pun intended) upstream? The forest managers have the onerous and delicate task of balancing these various uses of our forests.

Occasionally, certain sections of the forest can be designed for a particular type of management, such as wilderness areas. Yet even within a designated wilderness, an array of activities can take place as long as none of them violate the legal mandates set forth in the Wilderness Act. Often people do not realize that grazing, hunting, fishing, and even mining can take place within official wilderness areas as long as specific requirements are met regarding motorized equipment.

Further complicating land management is the fact that the boundaries of the public land are often political decisions, not ecological realities. These "islands" are greatly influenced by the neighboring national forest and private lands and even from above by commercial and private flights and air and noise pollution.

Native and non-native (primarily livestock) animals move fairly freely across these artificial boundaries – the animals' movements are a consequence of ecological parameters such as food and water availability, nesting sites, and evasion of predators. Plants, too, migrate (albeit much more slowly than animals) across the artificial boundaries.

A little over one hundred years ago, C. Hart Merriam recorded grizzly bears, wolves, bighorn sheep, and peregrine falcons as residents of the Red Rock–Sacred Mountain area. Those natives of the region are now just

memories, victims of overhunting and loss of habitat. The ever-increasing list of threatened, endangered, and extinct species speaks sadly of our poor relationship with the land and its native residents. Not only are plants and animals disappearing but traditional human lifeways are as well.

In 1905 the Michelbach family in Flagstaff was blessed with a baby boy. Pete Michelbach grew up living the cowboy life out on Hart Prairie; later his family's grazing land included a sizable chunk of the Red Rock–Sacred Mountain Country. Eighty-seven years later, despite a weathered tan face and rough, hard-worked hands, Pete looks and acts twenty years his junior. He winters in Sedona and summers on Hart Prairie. And he still tends his cattle, now spread across a number of different federal and state allotments, each one slowly becoming smaller as the Forest Service retires or trades certain acreage or the state sells holdings to developers.

On a warm, sunny morning last December, I met Pete at his winter place, a self-built room attached to an old mobile home squatting on ten acres in west Sedona. The man is something of a legend, well known to many. Sometimes so many people greet him in town that he has trouble remembering all those names and faces. From under his black cowboy hat, he grins, "If God doesn't know them any better than me, they're lost souls."

I hear tales about him taking a horse up the elevator in the Monte Vista Hotel in downtown Flagstaff and his first look at Oak Creek with a wild character named Matt Black; stories about the Dirty Brothers plus a barrel of hooch found on the lava beds and drunk down with gusto until the skeleton of a rat floated to the surface; adventures of herding cattle in blizzards and picking potatoes on Hart Prairie.

He tells me that when he bought this place in the 1950s there was nothing else around. But now he's surrounded by a housing development with a new house under construction less than a hundred feet away.

Like so many of the other native residents, Pete is an endangered species. His way of life has become essentially an anachronism. He says that he sees the little rancher going extinct but thinks that bigger outfits will absorb the smaller plots of grazing land and either put cattle on them or build golf courses. He also feels it was the big outfits that abused the land; the smaller ranchers had a better understanding of the land and a sincere desire to keep it productive for future generations.

Change is inevitable. Ecological systems are never at rest. They are always changing – dynamic equilibrium may be reached (e.g., a climax forest) but that too will change. Nothing lasts forever. Ecosystems – indeed, the rocky

The lofty San Francisco Peaks cast their spell upon all who pass near.

116

landscape itself—are temporal. We can only hope that we will never lose sight of our roots to the earth, our dependency on the earth for air, food, and water. Ultimately, and selfishly, the wise management of our natural resources translates as the sustenance of our lives. The continued disruption and disdain of natural ecosystems not only degrades human life but portends the eventual demise of this arrogant mammal.

The fragmentation of the land into parks and wilderness areas is not the ultimate solution to wise management of our resources. Nor are additional laws to protect endangered species of value unless our culture perceives the earth as a precious resource in our care, not just a commodity.

Slowly we are beginning to realize the dimensions of ecosystems. For example, as grand as Yellowstone National Park is, only in the past decade or two have we begun to realize that the Yellowstone ecosystem goes far beyond the artificial political boundaries of the park. Likewise, the Grand Canyon seems inviolate from a viewpoint high on the South Rim, but its life blood, the Colorado River, has been dramatically altered by dams outside of the park and the canyon's air fouled by distant power plants and traffic. The Red Rock–Sacred Mountain region cannot be perpetuated by setting aside islands of small parks; nice as they are, they are not ecologically self-sustaining. The bigger picture must be taken into account.

Intangible, spiritual qualities of the land must also be considered. A number of years ago, a meeting took place between the Forest Service and traditional Native American religious leaders. The Forest Service was being petitioned by the owners of the downhill ski resort on the Peaks to allow further expansion of their facilities. An upwelling of protest emerged from Native Americans who hold the mountain as sacred.

Hopi, Navajo, Zuni, and Apache mounted a legal battle to block the development on the grounds that the facility infringed on their religious freedom.

At this particular meeting, one of the forest rangers asked the Hopi: "Just show us on this map which parts of the mountain are sacred so that we can protect them." Of course, the Hopi were incredulous. They tried to explain, "How can we point on a map to a sacred place? The entire mountain, the land surrounding the mountain, the whole earth is sacred." Obviously such radically different viewpoints rarely lead to satisfying compromises.

The not-unexpected outcome was that the U.S. Circuit Court of Appeals in Washington, D.C., rejected the Native Americans' First Amendment religious freedom argument and ruled that the Forest Service had taken

precautions to protect the Peaks environment. The ski area was developed more, with some restrictions and with free lift rides available to Hopi and Navajo medicine men.

Too often when wildlife or traditional values are pitted against "progress" and "economic" considerations, they lose.

But there may be hope. Jim Ruch, executive vice president of the Grand Canyon Trust, a conservation organization dedicated to wise use of the public lands and natural resources of the Colorado Plateau, envisions the Sedona-Flagstaff area becoming a national recreation area. He believes: "The social and economic uses of the land are changing. The timber and cattle industries are declining on the public lands and recreation and tourism are growing. Flagstaff sits in a unique situation; it's the largest community on the Colorado Plateau, totally enclosed by national forest, is at the intersection of two major interstates, has railroad, bus, and airplane facilities, national parks nearby, dramatic cultural history and contemporary native peoples, and an existing tourist infrastructure. Combine these attributes with the spectacular scenery and wide diversity of habitats and you can see that we really have something very special here.

"Not only would tourists come to see and learn about the natural and cultural attributes of the area, tours could be arranged to show people how the public land is used and managed. Tours of logging operations and cattle ranches would not only educate the visitor where lumber and steaks come from but could possibly serve as a monitor to the timber and cattle industries."

The lofty San Francisco Peaks continue to cast their alluring spell, touching and influencing the lives of those who pass near. The Red Rock Country continues to be mysterious. Through time, Indians, surveyors, pioneers, and scientists alike have been drawn to the Red Rock–Sacred Mountain region. The mountains and canyons still command our attention and respect, inspire spiritual wonder, and spark scientific curiosity. When the weary traveler's eyes first glimpse the distinctive silhouette of the Peaks on the horizon or the red spires and cliffs near Oak Creek, the heart warms with the knowledge that home is not far away. The Peaks remain a constant on the landscape of our fast-paced lives and provide solace to those within the shadow of the mountain's shoulder. The red rocks speak of warm sunsets and glorious vistas.

Last night I was once again at Bell Rock, this time at night, taking long exposure photos of the butte silhouetted against the stars. A nearly continuous stream of cars raced by on the highway. Ironically, I was standing within a designated wilderness area but could hear only traffic

According to believers in the New Age philosophy, Bell Rock, a few miles south of Sedona, is one of several sites of mystical energy vortexes in the Red Rock Country.

118

Above: The Sedona District forest rangers are concerned about "the coming of the New Age." Some uninformed proponents of New Age philosophy are building permanent medicine wheels and other stone structures on national forest land, which is not permitted. And occasionally ancient petroglyphs and ruins are defaced by over-zealous New Agers. Left: The ever-increasing numbers of residents and visitors and their attendant use and abuse of the Red Rock–Sacred Mountain area's natural resources contribute to the degradation of the ecosystem. Above right: Modern developments and urbanization threaten prehistoric sites, most of which are still considered sacred by Native Americans. Overleaf: The sweep of the Red Rock Country beguiles the visitor.

noise and was bothered by the play of headlights on the red rocks.

Since my first, quiet night-time trip through Oak Creek Canyon, the permanent and tourist population of the Red Rock–Sacred Mountain area has grown phenomenally. Nearly all the woes facing this country can be linked to too many people asking too much from the land and its resources. We must learn, and soon, that we are all connected to our natural world.

I find it hard to fathom the point of view expressed by so many of our governmental leaders, recently expressed by Jack Kemp, secretary of Housing and Urban Development: "People are not a drain on the resources of the planet." Do our politicians not realize that we live on a planet of finite, albeit recyclable, assets? The people keep coming. According to the New Age believers, there may be a supernatural intervention or aliens to rescue us from ourselves, but if the Mothership is coming tonight, it might have to wait for a parking place.

Pinyon pines produce tasty, nutritious nuts that have been highly prized by Native Americans for thousands of years and today command exorbitant prices at the grocery store.

FURTHER READING

Many books, articles, and unpublished sources were read during the preparation of this book. Due to space limitations, this reading list contains only a few of these sources, particularly those that should be readily available in most large libraries.

General Reading and Guidebooks

Aitchison, Stewart. 1978. *Oak Creek Canyon and the Red Rock Canyon of Arizona: A Natural History and Trail Guide.* Flagstaff, AZ: Stillwater Canyon Press.

———. 1989. *A Guide to Exploring Oak Creek and the Sedona Area.* Salt Lake City, UT: RNM Press.

Aitchison, Stewart, and Bruce Grubbs, eds. 1991. *A Hiker's Guide to Arizona.* Helena, MT: Falcon Press Publishing Co., Inc.

Grey, Zane. 1924. *Call of the Canyon.* New York, NY: Simon & Schuster, Inc.

Weir, Bill. 1986. *Arizona Handbook.* Chico, CA: Moon Publications.

Ancient Seas & Lava Rivers

Breed, William J. 1985. "The San Francisco Peaks: A Geologist's Perspective." *Plateau* 56 (3):24–32.

Chronic, Halka. 1983. *Roadside Geology of Arizona.* Missoula, MT: Mountain Press Publishing Company.

Colton, Harold S., and Frank C. Baxter. 1932. *Days on the Painted Desert and the San Francisco Mountains: A Guide.* Flagstaff, AZ: Museum of Northern Arizona.

Middleton, Larry, and Richard Holm. 1987. "Erosion, Mesas, and Volcanoes." In *Earth Fire: A Hopi Legend of the Sunset Crater Eruption,* Ekkehart Malotki with Michael Lomatuway'ma. Flagstaff, AZ: Northland Press.

Nelson, Lisa. 1990. *Ice Age Mammals of the Colorado Plateau.* Flagstaff, AZ: Northern Arizona University Press.

Pewe, T. L., and R. G. Updike. 1976. *San Francisco Peaks: A Guidebook to the Geology.* 2d ed. Flagstaff, AZ: Museum of Northern Arizona.

Ranney, Wayne. 1989. "The Verde Valley: A Geological History." *Plateau* 60 (3):1–32.

Robinson, Henry H. 1913. *The San Francisco Volcanic Field, Arizona.* Washington, DC: Washington Printing Office, U.S.G.S. Professional Paper 76.

Smiley, Terah L., J. Dale Nations, Troy L. Pewe, John P. Schafer, eds. 1984. *Landscapes of Arizona: The Geological Story.* Lanham, MD: University Press of America.

People Without Water

Agenbroad, Larry D. 1990. "Before the Anasazi." *Plateau* 61 (2):1–32.

Bennett, Gary. 1988. "Burial of the Magician." *Arizona Highways* 64 (8):10–13.

Downum, Christian E. 1992. "The Sinagua." *Plateau* 63(1):1–32.

Hodge, Carle. 1986. *Ruins Along the River.* Tucson, AZ: Southwest Parks and Monuments Association.

Khera, Sigrid, and Patricia S. Mariella. 1983. "Yavapai." In *Handbook of North American Indians.* Vol. 10. Washington, DC: Smithsonian Institution.

Pilles, Peter J., Jr. 1979. "Sunset Crater and the Sinagua: A New Interpretation." In *Volcanic Activity and Human Ecology,* eds. Payson D. Sheets and Donald K. Grayson. New York, NY: Academic Press.

———. 1981. "The Southern Sinagua." *Plateau* 53 (1):6–17.

———. 1987a. "Hisatsinom: The Ancient People." In *Earth Fire: A Hopi Legend of the Sunset Crater Eruption,* Ekkehart Malotki with Michael Lomatuway'ma. Flagstaff, AZ: Northland Press.

———. 1987b. "The Sinagua: Ancient People of the Flagstaff Region." In *Wupatki and Walnut Canyon: New Perspectives on History, Prehistory, Rock Art. Exploration,* Annual Bulletin of the School of American Research. Santa Fe, NM: School of American Research.

Schroeder, Albert H. 1974. *Yavapai Indians: A Study of Yavapai History.* New York, NY: Garland Publishing Company.

Stein, Pat. 1981. "The Yavapai and Tonto Apache." *Plateau* 53 (1):18–23.

Thybony, Scott. 1987. *Fire and Stone.* Tucson, AZ: Southwest Parks and Monuments Association.

———. 1988. *Walnut Canyon.* Tucson, AZ: Southwest Parks and Monuments Association.

Explorers & Scientists

Babbitt, James E. 1981. "Surveyors Along the 35th Parallel: Alexander Gardner's Photographs of Northern Arizona, 1867–1868." *The Journal of Arizona History* 22 (3):325–48.

Byrkit, James. 1988. "The Palatkwapi Trail." *Plateau* 59 (4):1–32.

Cline, Platt. 1976. *They Came to the Mountain: The Story of Flagstaff's Beginnings.* Flagstaff, AZ: Northern Arizona University with Northland Press.

Fewkes, J. Walter. 1896a. "Two Ruins Recently Discovered in the Red Rock Country, Arizona." *American Anthropologist* 9 (8):263–84.

———. 1896b. "Preliminary Account of an Expedition to the Cliff Houses of the Red Rock Country, and the Tusayan Ruins of Sikyatki and Awatobi, Arizona, in 1895." *Annual Report of the Smithsonian Institution for 1895.* Washington, DC: Government Printing Office.

———. 1912. "Antiquities of the Upper Verde and Walnut Creek Valleys, Arizona." *Twenty-eighth Annual Report of the Bureau of American Ethnology.* Washington, DC: Government Printing Office.

Houk, Rose. 1991. *From the Hill: The Story of Lowell Observatory.* Flagstaff, AZ: Lowell Observatory.

Howard, William. 1981. *Sedona Reflections . . . Tales of Then for Now.* Sedona, AZ: Pronto Press.

Lowell, A. Lawrence. 1935. *Biography of Percival Lowell*. New York, NY: The MacMillan Company.

Lowell, Percival. 1910. *Mars as the Abode of Life*. New York, NY: The MacMillan Company.

McBride, Laura Purtymun. 1980. *Traveling by Tin Lizzie: The Great Model T Road Trip of 1924*. Sedona, AZ: Pronto Press.

Miller, Jimmy H. 1985. "A Philadelphia Brahmin in Flagstaff: The Life of Harold Sellers Colton." Ph.D. diss., Northern Arizona University, Flagstaff, AZ.

Mollhausen, Baldwin. 1858. *Diary of a Journey from the Mississippi to the Coasts of the Pacific, with a United States Government Expedition*. London, England.

Sedona Westerners. 1975. *Those Early Days . . . Old Timer's Memoirs*. Cottonwood, AZ: The Verde Independent.

Sitgreaves, Lorenzo. 1853. *Report of an Expedition Down the Zuni and Colorado Rivers, 1851*. 33rd Congress, 1st Session, Senate Executive Document, No. 59, Washington, DC.

Webb, George. 1983. *Tree Rings and Telescopes: The Scientific Career of A. E. Douglass*. Tucson, AZ: University of Arizona Press.

Whipple, Amiel W. 1856. *Report of Explorations for a Railroad Route Near the 35th Parallel of N. Latitude from the Mississippi to the Pacific Ocean*. Vol. 3, Pacific Survey Reports, 33rd Congress, 2nd Session, Senate Executive Document, No. 78, Washington, DC.

Life Zones

Aitchison, Stewart. 1985. "The San Francisco Peaks: A Biological Sky-Island." *Plateau* 56 (3):2–9.

Bailey, Vernon. 1889. Personal Letters to family and friends, written during the San Francisco Peaks Expedition. Housed at the American Heritage Center, University of Wyoming, Laramie. Copies on file at the Museum of Northern Arizona.

Merriam, C. H. 1890. "Results of a Biological Survey of the San Francisco Mountain Region and Desert of the Little Colorado in Arizona." *North American Fauna, #3*. Washington, DC: U.S. Department of Agriculture.

Phillips, Arthur M., III, Dorothy A. House, Barbara G. Phillips. 1989. "Expedition to the San Francisco Peaks." *Plateau* 60 (2):1–32.

Sterling, K. B. 1974a. *Last of the Naturalists: The Career of C. Hart Merriam*. New York, NY: Arno Press.

———. 1974b. *Selected Works of Clinton Hart Merriam*. New York, NY: Arno Press.

Whittaker, R. H. 1970. *Communities and Ecosystems*. New York, NY: The Macmillan Company.

Squirrels, Pines & Truffles

Allred, W. S. 1989. *Effects of Abert Squirrel Herbivory of Ponderosa Pine*. Ph.D. diss., Northern Arizona University, Flagstaff, AZ.

Austin, W. S. 1990. *Foraging Ecology and Behavior of Abert Squirrels*. Ph.D. diss., Northern Arizona University, Flagstaff, AZ.

Brown, David E. 1984. *Arizona's Tree Squirrel*. Phoenix, AZ: Arizona Game and Fish Department.

Lanner, Ronald M. 1984. *Trees of the Great Basin: A Natural History*. Reno, NV: University of Nevada Press.

Pielou, E. C. 1988. *The World of Northern Evergreens*. Ithaca, NY: Comstock Publishing Associates.

Sanford, Colleen. 1980. *Food Habits and Related Behavior of Abert Squirrels*. M.S. thesis, Northern Arizona University, Flagstaff, AZ.

States, Jack S. 1990. *Mushrooms and Truffles of the Southwest*. Tucson, AZ: University of Arizona Press.

Vireday, Carol. 1980. *Mycophagy in Tassel-eared Squirrels,* Sciurus aberti aberti *and* S. aberti kaibabensis *in Northern Arizona*. M.S. thesis, Northern Arizona University, Flagstaff, AZ.

Vanishing Old Growth

Crocker-Bedford, D. Coleman. 1990. "Goshawk Reproduction and Forest Management." *Wildlife Society Bulletin* 18 (3):262–69.

Dargan, Cecelia. 1992. *Mexican Spotted Owl Surveys: 1991*. Coconino National Forest, Flagstaff, AZ.

Forest Service. 1987. *Coconino National Forest Plan*. United States Department of Agriculture, Southwest Region, Albuquerque, NM.

Ganey, Joseph L. 1988. *Distribution and Habitat Ecology of Mexican Spotted Owls in Arizona*. M.S. thesis, Northern Arizona University, Flagstaff, AZ.

Ganey, Joseph L., and Russell Balda. 1989. "Distribution and Habitat Use of Mexican Spotted Owls in Arizona." *Condor* 91:355–61.

Nagiller, Sandra J., and Tamera K. Randall. 1988. *Spotted Owl Surveys: 1988–Coconino National Forest*. U.S. Fish and Wildlife Service and the U.S. Forest Service, Flagstaff, AZ.

Norse, Elliott A. 1990. *Ancient Forests of the Pacific Northwest*. Washington, DC: Island Press.

Ring, Ray. 1985. "One Man's Indictment of Forestry in Arizona." *High Country News,* Nov. 11, 10–13.

Suckling, Kieren. 1991. *Stone Forest Industries: An Initial Report to the People and Commission of Catron County*. Unpublished report prepared for Catron County Commission, NM.

Tolan, Mary. 1991. "Taking Stands in the Pines." *Phoenix* 26 (12):100–108.

———. 1992. "No One Sees the Trees or the Forest in Arizona's Old Growth." *Trilogy* 4 (1):68–73.

The Riparian Way

Carothers, Steven W., R. Roy Johnson, and Stewart W. Aitchison. 1974. "Population Structure and Social Organization of Southwestern Riparian Birds." *American Zoologist* 14:97–108.

Johnson, R. Roy, and Dale A. Jones, tech. coord. 1977. *Importance, Preservation and Management of Riparian Habitat: A Symposium*, USDA Forest Service, General Technical Report RM-43, Tucson, AZ.

Slingluff, Jim. 1990. *Verde River Recreation Guide*. Phoenix, AZ: Golden West Publishers.

Pygmy Forests

Betancourt, Julio L., Thomas R. VanDevender, and Paul S. Martin, eds. 1990. *Packrat Middens: The Last 40,000 Years of Biotic Change*. Tucson, AZ: University of Arizona Press.

Christensen, Kerry M., and Thomas G. Whitham. 1991. "Indirect Herbivore Mediation of Avian Seed Dispersal in Pinyon Pine." *Ecology* 72 (2):534–42.

Lanner, Ronald M. 1981. *The Piñon Pine: A Natural and Cultural History*. Reno, NV: University of Nevada Press.

Masters, Nancy Louise. 1979. *Breeding Birds of Pinyon-Juniper Woodland in North Central Arizona*. M.S. thesis, Northern Arizona University, Flagstaff, AZ.

Mopper, Susan, and Thomas G. Whitham. 1986. "Natural Bonsai of Sunset Crater." *Natural History* 95 (12):42–47.

O'Meara, T. E. 1978. *Effects of Chaining Pinyon-Juniper on Populations* of Rodents and Breeding Birds. M.S. thesis, Colorado State University, Fort Collins, CO.

Shewmaker, Joyce. 1987. *Fungal Consumption by the Arizona Gray Squirrel.* M.S. thesis, Northern Arizona University, Flagstaff, AZ.

Fire & Ice

Aitchison, Stewart. 1977. "Ice Worms." *Summit* 23 (4):6–9.
——. 1979a. "The Science of Snow." *Montana Magazine* 10 (2):16–18.
——. 1979b. "Snow: A Natural History." *Summit* 25 (1):7–11.
——. 1980. "How Animals Survive Winter." *Montana Magazine* 10 (3):9–11.

Cantor, Lisa F., and Thomas G. Whitham. 1989. "Importance of Below Ground Herbivory: Pocket Gophers May Limit Aspen to Rock Outcrop Refugia." *Ecology* 70 (4):962–70.

Kirk, Ruth. 1978. *Snow.* New York, NY: William Morrow & Co., Inc.

Lambert, Darwin, and David Muench. 1972. *Timberline Ancients.* Portland, OR: Charles H. Belding.

Pruitt, William O., Jr. 1967. *Animals of the North.* New York, NY: Harper & Row, Publishers.

Zwinger, Ann. 1970. *Beyond the Aspen Grove.* New York, NY: Random House.

A New Age?

Peterson, Natasha. 1988. *Sacred Sites: A Traveler's Guide to North America's Most Powerful, Mystical Landmarks.* Chicago & New York: Contemporary Books.

Sutphen, Dick. 1986. *Sedona: Psychic Energy Vortexes.* Malibu, CA: Valley of the Sun Publishing.

ORGANIZATIONS

These are a few of the organizations that help protect and study the natural history and cultural resources of the Red Rock–Sacred Mountain area.

The Arboretum at Flagstaff
P.O. Box 670, Flagstaff, AZ 86002
(602) 774-1441

Arizona Historical Society Pioneer Museum
Rt. 4, Flagstaff, AZ 86001
(602) 774-6272

Arizona Natural History Association
P.O. Box 1633, Flagstaff, AZ 86002
(602) 556-7474

Arizona State Parks:
Dead Horse State Park (602) 634-5283
Fort Verde State Historic Park (602) 567-3275
Jerome State Historic Park (602) 634-5381
Riordan State Historic Park (602) 779-4395
Red Rock State Park (602) 282-6907
Slide Rock State Park (602) 282-3034

Grand Canyon Trust
Rt. 4, Box 718, Flagstaff, AZ 86001
(602) 774-7488

Museum of Northern Arizona
Rt. 4, Box 720, Flagstaff, AZ 86001
(602) 774-5211

National Park Service:
Montezuma Castle National Monument (602) 567-3322
Sunset Crater National Monument (602) 527-7042
Tuzigoot National Monument (602) 634-5564
Walnut Canyon National Monument (602) 526-3367
Wupatki National Monument (602) 527-7040

Northern Arizona Audubon Society
P.O. Box 1496, Sedona, AZ 86336
(602) 284-9849

Sierra Club, Plateau Group
P.O. Box 15, Flagstaff, AZ 86002
(602) 774-1571

United States Forest Service, Coconino National Forest
2323 E. Greenlaw Lane, Flagstaff, AZ 86004
(602) 556-7400

ACKNOWLEDGMENTS

WRITING A BOOK IS a journey. When I began, I thought my twenty-seven years of living and working in the Red Rock–Sacred Mountain area had set me in good stead to write about the local natural history. But the farther along I got on this project, the more I realized that the body of scientific knowledge encompassing this area is overwhelming and continually being added to by researchers. Luckily, many selfless, helpful people guided me through this maze of knowledge. Although this book is done, my journey of learning continues.

Some of the kind folks who have given me new insight to the biology, geology, history, and politics of the Red Rock–Sacred Mountain area are: Charles Avery, James E. Babbitt, Russ Balda, Loyd Barnett, Ron Blakey, Bill Breed, Roger Clark, Wallace Covington, Dan Dagget, Cecelia Dargan, Fay Fisk, Sharon Galbreath, Joseph Ganey, Bob Gillies, Greg Goodwin, Heather Green, Dawson Henderson, Richard Holm, Rose Houk, Ken and Keen Jacobs, Al LeCount, Pete Michelbach, Rick Miller, Margaret Moore, John Nelson, Peter Pilles, Ron Plapp, Peter Price, Wayne Ranney, Jim Ruch, Jack States, Scott Thybony, Mary Tolan, Mike Wagner, Don Weaver, and Tom Whitham.

Over the years, countless individuals with the Forest Service have kindly provided advice and information. Besides the several already mentioned above, some of these people are: Joan Beno, Rod Byers, Bill Caskey, Bob Dyson, Holly Ennist, Vearl Haynes, Daryl Herman, Tom Holden, Skip Larson, Dennis Lund, Patrick McCoy, Nick McDonough, Sandra Nagiller, Neil Paulson, Barb Roberts, Walt Scott, Mike Sugaski, Garrish Willis, and Sam Wolfskill.

Pilots Bruce Grubbs and Michael Collier gave me a bird's-eye view of the Red Rock–Sacred Mountain Country. Tom Bean kindly taught me a few of his photographic secrets; and my long-time friend, Wild Bill Williams, has shared many memorable trail miles and ski adventures. A special thanks to Rick Reese who has been more influential on my writing than he may think.

I commend the staff at the Northern Arizona University Library, John Irwin and his staff at the Flagstaff Public Library, and Dotty House and her assistants at the Museum of Northern Arizona Library for their tireless efforts in helping me locate books and references.

For reading earlier versions of the manuscript, I would like to thank Betti Arnold Albrecht, Bruce Babbitt, Letty David, and David Maren. Bob DuBois, Helene Jones, Kathy Mallien, and the rest of the wonderful staff at Voyageur Press get the credit for putting all the pieces together. And finally, I want to thank my wife Ann for giving me the freedom and encouragement to write and my daughter Kate for taking long naps so Daddy could work at the computer.

One last note: I encourage you to read and listen to the many different perspectives of the natural history story. Obviously, it's a complex and evolving subject and one that is far from complete. Keep in mind, too, that while science searches for truths and produces facts and theories, all that information is then shaped by personal opinions and often applied (or disregarded) according to political agendas. In this book, all the opinions not cited and any errors of fact are totally my responsibility.

ABOUT THE
AUTHOR

Stewart Aitchison's writing and photography career grew out of his curiosity about the American Southwest's remarkable natural history. After graduating from Northern Arizona University, he went to work at the Museum of Northern Arizona as a research biologist. Presently, when not writing, he escorts natural history trips for Lindblad's Special Expeditions on the Colorado Plateau, Southeast Alaska, and Baja California. He is a member of the Authors Guild, Inc. and has written other books including: *A Wilderness Called Grand Canyon*, *A Guide to Exploring Oak Creek and the Sedona Area*, *A Hiker's Guide to Arizona* (with Bruce Grubbs), *A Naturalist's San Juan River Guide*, *A Naturalist's Guide to Hiking the Grand Canyon*, and *Utah Wildlands*. Aitchison makes his home in Flagstaff, Arizona, with his wife Ann and daughter Kate.

The famous red rock buttes, mesas, and cliffs of the Sedona area are composed primarily of the Schnebly Hill sandstone, which is rich in iron oxide.